No More Sheets

No More Sheets

Starting Over

Revised Edition

Juanita Bynum

DESTINY IMAGE® PUBLISHERS, INC.

P.O. Box 310, Shippensburg, PA 17257-0310

"Speaking to the Purposes of God for this Generation and for the Generations to Come."

This book and all other Destiny Image, Revival Press, MercyPlace, Fresh Bread, Destiny Image Fiction, and Treasure House books are available at Christian bookstores and distributors worldwide.

For a U.S. bookstore nearest you, call 1-800-722-6774.

For more information on foreign distributors, call 717-532-3040.

Or reach us on the Internet: www.destinyimage.com.

Hardcover ISBN: 0-7684-3278-2   978-0-7684-3278-7
Intl Trade Paper ISBN: 0-7684-3284-7   978-0-7684-3284-8
Large Print ISBN: 978-0-7684-3360-9
Ebook ISBN: 978-0-7684-9083-1

Previous Copyright © 1998 by Juanita Bynum ISBN 1-56229-126-2

Quote book ISBN 1-56229-154-8   Devotional ISBN 1-56229-149-1

For Worldwide Distribution, Printed in the U.S.A.

1 2 3 4 5 6 7 8 9 10 11 / 14 13 12 11 10

Dedication

I would like to dedicate this book to my niece, Lanita D. Laird. You have been my inspiration in writing this book. I wanted you to have an opportunity to live a full life and be completely happy and fulfilled as a single woman! I love you so much! When I saw some of the things you were going through, I had to help. And thanks for your golden typing fingers. We could not have finished this book without your skills!

I would like to also dedicate this book to Bishop Jakes, my coach. Thanks for not only believing in the ministry God has given me, but for having the guts to show it. Ha! Ha! Thanks for the hand up in ministry. You and your wife are forever in our prayers. There are no words to express my gratitude. Maybe when you get to Heaven, the Lord will reveal it to you, Bishop.

I also dedicate this book to my parents for putting everything that I needed in me to be able to start over!! Especially my dad I miss you sooo much!!!! And to my sister Alvina: Take care of Daddy up there, cause you know he's nosey (LOL). So keep him from getting thrown out of Heaven, please!! If he does, I would gladly take him back, right here with me; I love you guys. Wow; you and daddy are missed so much!!!

To Crystal Smith, there are no words in the English language to describe what you did for me!! No words! All I can say is, when I look at you and all you sacrificed and gave; I just saw God!! I saw God I believe as close as I will ever see Him in a person!! Thanks Crys. Thanks!!!

To the celebrity who's supported me, I will respect your privacy by not mentioning your name. All I can say is, I don't think I would have made it without my family!! Thanks.... thanks....thanks.

Special Thanks

To my staff, Edwina Johnson, Teshania Blackwell, Kimberly Thomas, Patrice Young, Madge Smith, Jerwan Young, Marie Swinson, Carla Mackey, Angela Gray, Alvina Clark, Cathy Brewington, Rena Sanderford, Tina Trice, Edith Woody, Bianca Simmons, Patrice Davis, and Nakeya Jones. You guys are the bomb!

To Rod Swinson and Tonya Swinson Hall, Goodness and Mercy. Guys, I pray that you both stay around for the rest of my life. One of these days, I am going to know that Bible like you guys do. Ha! Ha! Hanging around you two is like having the Bible on disk! Ha! Ha! The world has not heard of you two yet, but they will, and when they do, the nation will be blessed. Your season and time are coming!

Special, Special Thanks

To Pastors Terrell and Veter Nichols of Grand Rapids, Michigan, for cutting out the cancer of sexual sin.

To Pastor Donald and Gloria Alford, of Maywood, Illinois, for scraping it off.

To my pastor and father Dr. John, Sr. and Margie Boyd, of New Greater Bethel Ministries, my church home, for building me up and establishing my feet in my walk with the Lord and in wisdom.

To Pastor James Swinson and Johnnie May, for giving Juanita Bynum Ministries a home and for covering us in prayer. Thanks for the building, Pastor.

To Crystal Smith. There are no words in the English language to describe what you did for me!!! No words!!! All I can say is when I looked at you and all you sacrificed and gave, I just saw God!!!! I say God because I believe it is as close as I will ever be to seeing Him… in a person!!! Thanks Crys, Thanks!!!

Also, to Tuu (Crystal Power) and Tiff (Tiffany Caddell): Thanks for all of your support. Dr. Showell, thanks for all of your wisdom and support. Wow, what a journey, what a journey (LOL). Nevertheless, I was able to "start over" because of what you guys did for me. Thank you!

This Special, Special thanks page belongs to these people, and a dog. Butter, what can I say. No words can describe the joy and the love I get from you!!! The same love every single day.

To another, because of privacy I will give them the respect of not mentioning their name. All I can say is I don't think I would have made it without my Family!!! Thanks, Thanks, Thanks!

Why *No More Sheets?*

Why *No More Sheets?*

Because 70 percent of adolescents reported that they had experienced sexual intercourse by the age of 19. The pregnancy rate of sexually experienced females ages 15 to 19 is 7 percent and the abortion rate is 1.9 percent.[1] Nearly half of the 15- to 19-year-olds say they believe that the average adolescent today does not have enough accurate information about sex and reproduction.[2]

Why *No More Sheets?*

Because an estimated 333 million new cases of curable sexually transmitted diseases occur each year among adults. Of these, 3 million occur among teenagers, 13 to 19 years old. A recent CDC report documented that over 85 percent of the most common infectious diseases in the U.S. are sexually transmitted.[3]

Why *No More Sheets?*

Because HIV infection/AIDS has killed more than half a million people in the United States alone; the Center for Disease

Control estimates that 38,175 people age 20 to 24 have contracted AIDS through 2007; it estimates that in the United States, more than 9,000 children under 13 have AIDS.[4]

Why *No More Sheets*?

Because HIV/AIDS is a worldwide epidemic; according to a UNAIDS report, more than 33 million people are estimated to be living with HIV/AIDS; 25 million people have died from AIDS since the epidemic began in 1981. In Africa, over 14 million children have been made orphans because of AIDS.[5]

Why *No More Sheets*?

Because many people are trapped in a lifestyle of sexual sin—sin which some say is harmless. Pornography is a prime example. One study found that neighborhoods with a pornography business experienced 40 percent more property crime and 500 percent more sexual offenses than similar neighborhoods without a pornography outlet.[6] Eighty-six percent of convicted rapists said they were regular users of pornography.[7] Pornography is also a strong factor in the sexual abuse of children. Another study showed that 77 percent of those who molested boys and 87 percent of those who molested girls said they were regular users of hard-core pornography.[8]

Why *No More Sheets*?

Because sin will kill you.[9]

Why *No More Sheets*?

Because we perish for a lack of knowledge[10]: therefore, it's time to tell the truth about sex. The truth will make you free.[11]

Why *No More Sheets*?

The Starr Report.[12]

Endnotes

1. Centers for Disease Control and Prevention (CDC) report, *Sexual and Reproductive Health of Persons Aged 10–24 Years—United States, 2002–2007,* www. cdc.gov/mmwr/preview/mmwrhtml/ss5806a1. htm?s_cid=ss5806a1_e.

2. As reported by the Office of Population Affairs, U.S. Department of Health and Human Services, 1990.

3. Centers for Disease Control and Prevention (CDC) report, *The Challenge of STD Prevention in the United States,* November 1996.

4. Centers for Disease Control and Prevention (CDC) report, *HIV/AIDS Statistics and Surveillance,* Last Modified February 2009, http://www.cdc.gov/hiv/topics/surveillance/basic.htm.

5. AVERT, "Global HIV/AIDS Estimates, end of 2008," published by UNAIDS, November 2009, http://www.avert.org/worldstats.htm.

6. U.S. Department of Justice, *Child Pornography, Obscenity and Organized Crime,* February 1988.

7. W. Marshall, Use of Sexually Explicit Stimuli by Rapists, Child. Molesters and Non-Offenders, *Journal of Sex Research* 267, 1998.

8. W. Marshall, *Report on the Use of Pornography by Sexual Offenders,* Report to the Federal Department of Justice, Ottawa, Canada, 1983.

9. *"For the wages of sin is death; but the gift of God is eternal life through Jesus Christ our Lord"* (Romans 6:23).

10. *"My people are destroyed for lack of knowledge: because thou hast rejected knowledge, I will also reject thee, that thou shalt be no priest to Me: seeing thou hast forgotten the law of thy God, I will also forget thy children"* (Hosea 4:6).

11. *"And ye shall know the truth, and the truth shall make you free"* (John 8:32).

12. Independent Counsel, Kenneth W. Starr, headed an investigation that resulted in a report to Congress. The Starr Report alleged "substantial and credible information that President William Jefferson Clinton committed acts that may constitute grounds for an impeachment.... The evidence shows that these acts, and others, were part of a pattern that began as an effort to prevent the disclosure of information about the president's relationship with a former White House intern and employee, Monica S. Lewinsky, and continued as an effort to prevent the information from being disclosed in an ongoing criminal investigation." The White House rebuttal stated, "The President has confessed to indiscretions with Ms. Lewinsky...."

Contents

Foreword

Wow! Looking back over my shoulder, I am finding it hard to believe that it has been more than a decade since the message "No More Sheets" was preached. Although there is an introduction to the original manuscript for the book that followed, I deemed it necessary to add to the text by writing a foreword to what I believe is a timeless message.

I must admit, I wasn't prepared for what would come after I left that platform in 1998. It was as though this message grew its own legs and took off without me. When I looked up, it was everywhere. I couldn't walk anywhere—not the mall, not McDonald's, not the grocery store...nowhere! I couldn't move without somebody saying, "The 'No More Sheets' message changed my life."

I heard all kinds of variations of the message title: "Under the Covers"..."No More Blankets"..."Wrapped in the Sheets" (LOL)—you name it, and the people had a saying for what they experienced from listening to that message!

I have often said that if I had $100 for each time I have been told that "No More Sheets" changed somebody's life, I would be a billionaire! Ha!

The biggest shocker of all was that I had so many drug addicts tell me that they stopped shooting heroin after hearing the "No More Sheets" message. They told me, "I stopped cold turkey. I went through some tissues and when I got through following the crowd and cleaning myself off, I never touched drugs again!"

Beside heroin addicts, I couldn't begin to count the numbers of people who were instantly set free from crack cocaine. I shook my head in confusion, asking myself, "Wasn't this message about sex?"

As all of this began to take place and I began to receive so many different kinds of testimonies, I thought, *Wow. This isn't just about sex.* That's when it was revealed to me that the "No More Sheets" message and the spirit of the message were really about a bigger issue called *addiction*.

Can we take just a minute to look at the word *addiction?* It is the condition of being dependent on a particular substance, thing, or activity.

It all started to make sense: some people were addicted to substances, and some people were addicted to activities, and some were even addicted to people. That explains why, when I began to shout, "No more sheets!" in that auditorium, the place erupted. It was because a spirit of addiction was being broken off the lives of the people.

While doing further research, I found that to be addicted also means "to be dedicated or devoted to an obsession...to be infatuated with...to have passion for, or love of, a mania for." Another word popped up in my research, and this one really helped me to understand the uproar all over the world in response to this message: that word is *enslavement!*

When I say "all over the world," I mean all the places in the world I had been and even parts I had not visited—I mean, places I had never even heard of! Letters and phone calls came in saying, "After seeing the message 'No More Sheets,' my life will never be the same!"

People would walk up to me and say, "I saw the 'No More Sheets' message, Dr. Bynum, and I felt like that message brought freedom from mental slavery."

They were beginning to understand for the first time that they had been slaves to their own actions. It was being made clear that they had been slaves under other people's power. They were being made to realize that their lives were going in a direction that had nothing to do with true purpose or destiny.

All these people needed was to see one person make the stand and the rest would follow; it was like a domino effect. That was when I realized that the "No More Sheets" message had become an international sojourner of truth, a message that would lead many out of the clutches of mental, emotional, and physical slavery into a life of freedom like they had never experienced before—freedom to choose the abundant life.

This would be the key that would unlock the door of bondage no matter how deeply or how often the person felt ensnared by the enemy! This message would be the knife with the power to surgically remove diseases stemming from toxic relationships—the very "ailments" that have left many paralyzed and unable to move into their destinies.

This would be the message that even I would have to reach back to. I would have to digest its principles again—not just to save my life, but to restore my own soul, once again!

In looking back over the contents of the original text, I came to realize that the pages of this book may not provide *the* end-all answer for your life. However (as I have found to be true in my own life even now), it provided an avenue for me to engage in a dialogue within myself so that everything that had become disorganized (due to the decisions I have made) could be corrected!

This is the purpose of this book: to allow you, in the privacy of your own space, to take a good look at your addiction and break it!

One thing stands sure; after you realize that a decision you made was not necessarily the right one, you have the power and the right to press the "rewind" button and go back and do the work of restoration over again.

So here I am, one more time, naked and unashamed, but willing to turn my life's experience into a lesson in the hopes that millions behind me will never have to walk through the same fire I did! I realize and accept the responsibility of my decisions to the point of turning what looks like failure into a tool for success. I was woman enough to make the decision, and I will be woman enough to share the lesson.

I have often said to the millions of people I have been fortunate to teach over the past year: "This is your life. If you don't like it, change it!"

This is why I have chosen to add to this original man-uscript—so that every person reading this book would have the new opportunity to recognize the power lying dormant within them...the power to stand up and say, as I did: "I am starting over!"

Preface

No one knows how hard it was to write this book. I found it much more difficult than preaching the message. When you're flowing in a prophetic anointing and speaking spontaneously, as I was when "No More Sheets" was taped, you're not as concerned about what people will think.

The night I preached "No More Sheets," I didn't have a message planned. I only knew that God was going to use me. If you've seen the video, you know how drastically my life changed. I can't go back. That message exposed the intimate details of my life, so you can only imagine what I had to face while working on this book.

I didn't want to write just another inspirational book. I wanted to give people something honest and hard-hitting that would help them come to grips with themselves. I wanted to cut to the heart of relationship problems and sexual struggles that sidetrack many singles. Most of all, I wanted to help them get clean before God.

Many times I stopped writing because I had to forgive people and forgive myself for certain situations. I had gone through 15 or 20 years of cleansing my spirit. While writing the book, I had to relive *all* of those incidents. I constantly battled the enemy, who so desperately wanted to regain a foothold in my life. I had to close the door, barring unforgiveness from my heart.

You will never know my pain. I had to pause and put the book down for days. I said what I was able to say, but my inner woman felt what I couldn't say. I agonized over reliving my experiences, and I wept for joy that I'd been delivered. While you read this book, I invite you to pray for me, sincerely.

This book almost cost me my life. When I was within three days of finishing the project, I was in a car accident. I had just stopped by the cleaners to get some suits tailored—suits that I would wear to take photos for the cover of this book. On my way home, a young man ran a stop sign and hit me head on. His 1988 Oldsmobile knocked my little Volkswagen Beetle back half a block and into my neighbor's front yard. When I came to, I didn't know whether I was dead or alive. My brand-new car was totaled.

I know that the accident was directly related to this book being released. The enemy does not want God's people to be free emotionally, physically, or spiritually. He wants us to live as slaves to sex. Like many singles, you may have a preoccupation with it. But let me tell you, sex is highly overrated. This deceit ensnares many men and women, trapping them in bondage.

If you've jumped into the sheets and can't get out, there's hope. My life is a testimony that Jesus Christ is a deliverer who can cleanse you from any sin. You will have to work with God to accomplish your deliverance, but it can be done. If you want to stay free, then commit yourself to God's very best for your life and tell the devil, "There will be no more sheets!"

∞

WHEN WE BEGIN TO WORSHIP GOD,
WE MAKE OURSELVES SUSCEPTIBLE TO
THE CLEANSING POWER OF THE
HOLY SPIRIT.

∞

Introduction

As you read this book, you are not reading for information. You are not reading for entertainment. You are reading this book so that you can relocate your body parts. You are reading to find your identity.

I guarantee you that when you reach the last page of this book, you will have met the person you lost so long ago. You are going to find something very surprising. You are going to become reacquainted with who you really are and you are going to like who you see.

Are you wondering, "Why is she starting at the end of the message?" You might have been there when I preached this message. You may have seen the video. "Why is this woman starting at the end and working her way back to the beginning?"

My reason is simple. If I am going to be used of God, I must follow the pattern of God. Why do I say that? Because when Jesus died on the cross, the work was finished. We are complete in Him.

∽

WHO AND WHAT YOU ARE HAS ABSOLUTELY
NOTHING TO DO WITH WHAT YOU DO;
IT HAS EVERYTHING TO DO WITH
WHAT CHRIST HAS DONE.

∽

How an uncommon object or person was made is what makes it interesting. For instance, we look at the Statue of Liberty and admire her; but for me, I gained a different respect when I learned how she was made. Understanding that process afforded me the opportunity to never again take her beauty or her elegance for granted. Therefore, I invite you to take a death walk with me on the road to *No More Sheets.*

Before we go on that walk, I can hear someone say, "Why did all these things happen to me? Why was I molested as a child? Why was I sexually promiscuous? Why did I have so many partners? Why am I still with a partner and not yet satisfied?"

I have asked myself some of the same questions. One answer that I received in my spirit was this: somebody had to be Juanita Bynum, so it might as well be me. Now I want to give you the same words: somebody had to be you, so it might as well be you.

∽

NO MORE LIES, DECEIT, PAIN,
GRIEF, ABUSE, OR MISUSE.
NO MORE SHEETS!

∽

Trust me when I tell you that upon completing this walk with me, you will have become a better person. You will have done what a lot of people are afraid to do. You will have faced your past. You will have been exposed to the workings of satan and will no longer have to become vulnerable to his tactics because you will know the truth! For John 16:13 says, *"Howbeit when He, the Spirit of truth, is come, He will guide you into all truth..."* Therefore I say to you, follow me down the road to no more sheets!

CHAPTER ONE

What Did I Do Last Night?

I'm sitting on the side of the bed at about 7:30 in the morning, looking across the street from my hotel window. The flow of traffic and pedestrians gives this the appearance of a typical Sunday morning. As swiftly as the cars move down the road, the question rings in my mind over and over again: "What did I do last night?" This is the power and the pressure of the morning after.

"The morning after what?" you ask.

I feel the same thing I felt the morning after I failed God—the morning after I had sex with someone I was not married to.

Last night I didn't uncover myself with a man, but I stood before a crowd and bared my soul. I shared the intimate details of my life with single men and women who have likewise been trapped in unholy relationships. It was necessary for my wounds to be reopened. I died a slow and painful death in front of those people so someone else could live again.

No one knows how I feel right now. My workers are all in their rooms. My mother is in Chicago taking care of my father who is sick. That means I have to face the trauma and thoughts of the morning after all by myself.

My mind asks, "What are people saying? What are they thinking? Did the people receive? Had the Word been rejected?" I knew that I had told it all. I bared my soul. I also asked myself, "Lord, how painful must this get? How far does this process go?"

OK, so I did the tape. I did the video. Why am I still feeling such mixed emotions? I feel somewhat embarrassed. I feel somewhat alone. I feel exposed and vulnerable. Yet, at the same time, I am still not satisfied. Am I crazy? With all these feelings, I still felt that there was more that I needed to say. That's one reason I felt compelled to write this book.

Yes, it was difficult for me to do what I did. But when I speak to a crowd, God lets me see beneath the makeup, jewelry, and stylish clothes. When I see a soul at war with its own body, I have to do something. I say to myself, "I must help!" I am only experiencing a fraction of what Jesus must have felt when He looked out and said to His Father, "Who shall go?" Just as Jesus said, so say I, "Father, send me. I will go!"

Answering My Mandate

Pastors, friends, and colleagues told me how powerful the video and the message were. They insisted that I write this book because I would really get paid. But you know what? Juanita Bynum's message is not about a market; it's a mandate.

That morning, as I peeled myself out of the bed, I felt unsure of what I would face behind those closed doors. The maid knocked, and I thought it was one of my workers. I said to myself, "How can I show my face? Oh my God, I just can't do this!"

I knew that I had to face my tomorrow, just as everyone else did. But for some reason, by the time I got dressed and stood in front of the bathroom mirror, I was more beautiful to myself than I had ever been in my life. I felt a sense of renewing. I felt I had been emptied out. Surprisingly, I felt free!

As I walked down the hall, my workers were in silence. No one knew what to say. Finally, as we entered the elevator, one worker whose eyes were torn between looking at me and looking at the floor, spoke with a shaking, quivering voice and said, "Prophetess, you set me free."

At that moment, as the elevator began to descend, I knew it was worth it all. For one person to say that to me, I felt like I got paid. For a worker within my own camp to say, "You set me free," that was payment enough! I had no clue what kind of impact last night's message had made on the audience. In a matter of minutes, however, I would discover just how deeply people had been touched.

Our Story

As the elevator door opened, the lobby was filled with people coming from the morning service at Bishop Jakes' church. Some were going and some were coming. I hurried through the lobby, barely being recognized by anyone before I exited the building.

Finally, the dreaded moment came when I stopped moving. As I waited at the curb for the security guards to bring the car around, a young woman jumped out of a car, ran over to me, and buried her head in my bosom. She wept and whimpered, "No more sheets!" Another woman embraced me and said, "I'm about to catch my plane, and I got some stuff I have to throw out of my house."

By the time the car arrived, six or seven people were standing there holding on to me and saying, "Prophetess, thank you. Thank you so much for telling *our* story." Those words hit my spirit so hard. Standing on that curb, I realized it was not my story; it was our story. I was just the sacrifice to the public, but it was the story of millions of people.

That's the secret to *No More Sheets*. It's not the Juanita Bynum story. It's the story of every woman and man in the Body of Christ who has no platform. That day, I spoke for every person who wanted to be free. I became all of the voices crying out in silence—voices no one has ever heard. I became every groan, moan, heartbreak, disappointment, and molestation. I became that person. I was the voice of the people crying out to God saying, "Bring me out of the sheets!"

As the car drove away and the people waved and wept, I didn't feel like a star. I had only done what God had asked me to do. I had assisted Him in saving a soul. By motivating one or two or three to walk in integrity and righteousness, I was helping one more person to present his or her body a living sacrifice. When I got to church, I walked in proud. My head was held high, not because I was Prophetess Bynum, but because I had helped somebody!

I have preached a lot of messages. I have ministered in a number of places, but that day on the platform, I answered my mandate—*no more sheets!*

Why Sheets?

Maybe you weren't in the audience that day. You may never have heard the tape or seen the video. You may be wondering,

"What are these sheets she's talking about?" Well, my friend, sheets are layers of bondage that have affected your emotions through sexual experiences.

A lot of single men and women are bound up today. Sisters are carrying the baggage of past relationships and sexual encounters. Brothers aren't free to answer God's call on their lives. Weighed down with guilt, shame, and regret, these believers have become ineffective for the Kingdom.

∞

SISTERS ARE CARRYING THE BAGGAGE
OF PAST RELATIONSHIPS…AND
BROTHERS AREN'T FREE TO ANSWER
GOD'S CALL. WEIGHED DOWN…THEY
HAVE BECOME INEFFECTIVE FOR
THE KINGDOM.

∞

When I tied three sheets around my waist and continued to preach, it was hard to move around the platform. I kept hoping that they wouldn't catch on something. You see, sheets will affect your walk with God.

Don't think you're exempt because you're a Christian. If you jumped in and out of the sheets with someone who was not your spouse, those sexual experiences have bound you up. It will take work to get free, and you are going to need some help! Let's go to a passage from the Bible:

And when He [Jesus] thus had spoken, He cried with a loud voice, Lazarus, come forth. And he that was dead came forth, bound hand and foot with graveclothes: and his face was bound about with a napkin. Jesus saith unto them, Loose him, and let him go (John 11:43-44).

33

Yes, you may be born again. You may have experienced resurrection power. But you may be unable to enjoy the blessings of God because of those sheets. Like Lazarus, you need those grave clothes to loose you and let you go.

Having been in the sheets, I know the emotional devastation they can cause. Gradually, however, you become comfortable with them. You may have been wrapped in them so long that you can't imagine life any other way. But if you want to enjoy the fullness of God, you must cast off those sheets. You must make this declaration for every future relationship: No more sheets!

Over the years, God has shown me how to rid myself of layers of sheets that had affected my work for Him. It was a painful process. I learned the hard way, but you don't have to. You can hasten the healing in your own life by gleaning from my experience.

∞

IF YOU WANT TO ENJOY THE FULLNESS
OF GOD, YOU MUST CAST OFF THOSE
SHEETS AND DECLARE FOR EVERY
FUTURE RELATIONSHIP:
"NO MORE SHEETS!"

∞

It's in the Bible!

The whole concept of *No More Sheets* is based on a husband and a wife knowing each other and becoming "one flesh." That is stated in the Old Testament:

Therefore shall a man leave his father and his mother, and shall cleave unto his wife: and they shall be one flesh (Genesis 2:24).

Today we go through a marriage ceremony just for the sake of saying, "I'm married." The spoken vow is not as important as it once was. In Bible days, your word was your bond.

If a father gave his daughter to a man who vowed to take her as his wife, and the man had intercourse with the daughter, that marriage was consummated.

If any man take a wife, and go in unto her, and hate her, and give occasions of speech against her, and bring up an evil name upon her, and say, I took this woman, and when I came to her, I found her not a maid: then shall the father of the damsel, and her mother, take and bring forth the tokens of the damsel's virginity unto the elders of the city in the gate: and the damsel's father shall say unto the elders, I gave my daughter unto this man to wife, and he hateth her; and, lo, he hath given occasions of speech against her, saying, I found not thy daughter a maid; and yet these are the tokens of my daughter's virginity. And they shall spread the cloth before the elders of the city. And the elders of that city shall take that man and chastise him; and they shall amerce him in an hundred shekels of silver, and give them unto the father of the damsel, because he hath brought up an evil name upon a virgin of Israel: and she shall be his wife; he may not put her away all his days (Deuteronomy 22:13-19).

Apparently, a man would desire a woman, take her virginity, then lie and say she was not a virgin. That was his way of getting out of that relationship. He was now free to sleep with someone else. The father brought the sheets to the judges. If there was blood on the sheets caused by the woman's hymen breaking during intercourse, then the man had taken her virginity.

When I preached the message "No More Sheets," I was not even aware of that passage. A year later, a bishop gave me this scriptural base for my message.

The Lord told me that there will be no more sheets. There will be no more acts in which men lay down with women and shed blood on the sheets without vowing to stay with them for life. This has to cease in the Body of Christ.

Deuteronomy 12:19 says that the power of intercourse was such that once a man had slept with the woman, he was not allowed to put her away...ever.

That law still stands today. We cannot take intercourse lightly. It is an act of covenant, an act of marriage that joins two souls together. That's where we get the term *soul ties*.

⬡

WHEN YOU ENGAGE IN INTERCOURSE
WITH SOMEONE, YOUR SOULS BECOME
ENTWINED. YOUR EMOTIONS AND
THOUGHTS TAKE ON THE WILL OF
THAT PERSON.

⬡

When a man enters your body, he comes to stay. You and he are one. We take that for granted. When a man has intercourse with you, he adds his life to yours. When he leaves, his body is no longer there, but his spirit is; you are left with only the weight of the memory. The woman is left devastated. It's as if someone walks out of your life, splits you in half, and then says, "Just go your own way." That's why there is such a cry from the realm of the spirit—no more sheets!

❧

STOP PROLONGING YOUR PAST AND CUT THE TIE THAT BINDS YOU TO THAT SOUL.

❧

Removing My Fig Leaves

Preaching this message on video made me feel like the subject of a global autopsy. I candidly revealed the reason behind my sheets. But today, I can hear the voice of my Master walking through the garden of my experiences, telling me to remove my fig leaves and reveal the naked truth, just as He told Adam and Eve:

> *And they heard the voice of the Lord God walking in the garden in the cool of the day: and Adam and his wife hid themselves from the presence of the Lord God amongst the trees of the garden. And the Lord called unto Adam, and said unto him, Where art thou? And he said, I heard Thy voice in the garden, and I was afraid, because I was naked; and I hid myself* (Genesis 3:8-10).

I can hear the voice of the Lord thundering in my spirit, saying, "Juanita, tell them where you are." This is not easy for me. Why? Because the fig leaves have done a pretty good job of concealing my shame. But in order for me to help others remove their fig leaves and be healed, I must first remove mine.

Are you wondering if this is just another message to singles? No, this is a message to the world! If you are single, so am I. If you have been married, so have I. If you have been divorced, so have I. If you have been wounded, so have I. If you have been lonely, so have I. If you have fallen, so have I. I believe I have borne enough scars to help you with yours.

Until we have survived a war, we can't preach about war. Until we have survived broken marriages, we really can't help anyone else through a divorce. Only a person who is surviving the sting of being single can really elaborate on the plight of singles.

Tell Your Story

Do you realize the type of ministry that the Lord is taking us into today? We have to embrace reality. Phoniness won't cut it. Facades won't do. Image is not where it's at. If the Church doesn't get real, we're going to lose a whole lot of folks, and that's a fact.

❧

PHONINESS WON'T CUT IT. IF THE
CHURCH DOESN'T GET REAL, WE'RE
GOING TO LOSE A WHOLE LOT
OF FOLKS.

❧

I know by the Holy Spirit that all who intend to minister and stand as spiritual giants in this hour will hit a brick wall. You may be able to preach the Scriptures, but one day, you will have to stand on a platform and tell not just Daniel's story of surviving the lions' den, but your own.

In the beginning was the Word, and the Word was with God, and the Word was God. The same was in the beginning with God. All things were made by Him; and without

Him was not any thing made that was made....And the Word was made flesh, and dwelt among us, (and we beheld His glory, the glory as of the only begotten of the Father,) full of grace and truth (John 1:1-3,14).

We understand that the Word was made flesh. Jesus exemplified that Scripture. Eventually, He stopped speaking with His mouth, and His actions told His story. When Jesus went into the grave and got up the third day, He was respected as having all power. Because He had lived a sinless life and yet bore our embarrassment and shame, He could become the Savior of the world.

Our mandate is not just to save the world. Every minister, prophet, and teacher has been given a people. You are responsible to tell your story to your people so that they can know the power of God. One of the most powerful tools that anybody can use is his or her testimony.

The power of God is the anointing that destroys every yoke. We entertain people, but yokes are not being destroyed. When I leave the platform, I want to know that I didn't just excite people, but that I really helped them! The Word tells us:

And it shall come to pass in that day, that his burden shall be taken away from off thy shoulder, and his yoke from off thy neck, and the yoke shall be destroyed because of the anointing (Isaiah 10:27).

Someone who has survived the experience can destroy a yoke. Surviving the experience increases the anointing on your life in that area. Sharing your own testimony of the power of God will set others free. If you dare to step out in faith and be transparent, I believe you will find the bridge that leads you into a more liberated life.

∞

ONE OF THE MOST POWERFUL TOOLS
YOU CAN USE IS YOUR ABILITY TO
TESTIFY.

∞

You see, sin is so prevalent that preaching about Daniel and then comparing him to yourself becomes even more of a necessity. You can say, "Look at me. I was in a den, but the Lord shut the mouth of those lions. Now I am free." My friend, your testimony helps others grasp the supernatural works of God.

In this hour, people want to hear how *you* got out. Tell me how you came through. Many ministers may be reading this book and saying, "But Prophetess Bynum, I can't speak on it because I am still going through."

Do you know what I would say to you? Jesus' crucifixion showed us that He can relate to our struggles and pain; but His rising from the grave is what made me believe in resurrection power. When you tell someone, "I'm striving to live for God just like you," there's power in that. You're not only helping them to walk in victory, but you're also showing someone else how to walk in faith! The Word says this:

> *But they that wait upon the Lord shall renew their strength;*
> *they shall mount up with wings as eagles; they shall run,*
> *and not be weary; and they shall walk, and not faint*
> (Isaiah 40:31).

When you wait upon the Lord, your strength is renewed. You are not in a powerless position; you are in a position of being empowered. When you come through this, your experience will snap the yoke off somebody else's neck. Your experience will mend a marriage. You may be asking, "Should I bare my heart and tell all?" No, many people could never understand your whole testimony, but there is a part of your life that you need to share that will bring deliverance.

∾

IT MAY NOT BE EASY, BUT YOU'VE GOT TO WAIT ON THE LORD.

∾

People have asked me about being embarrassed. I believe that a woman is embarrassed by her bondage. When you are free, you are glad to come out. Like the woman at the well, you drop everything and tell the city that you met a man who told you everything about yourself. We fight too hard to maintain an image!

The Word says that if you seek to save your life, you will lose it. If you lose it for His sake, however, you gain. Daily, Jesus lost His reputation. He was controversial. He opposed the religious system of His day, disrupting the status quo of the scribes and Pharisees. He had a mandate on His life that demanded attention.

Yet, we say that we want to be like Jesus! No, I beg to differ with you. Our fleshly desire is not to be like Jesus; we want to conform to the system.

In order to be used in this hour, a person who has a mandate—not just a ministry—must be freed from the political aspects of ministry. He or she must also be freed on a daily basis from what people think and say. A bishop called to say that the message, "No More Sheets" was not of God. What do I think about that? *If this message is not of God, then I want to thank the devil for setting so many people free!*

I would not insult your intelligence by telling you a fictitious story about how I made it over, all the while still lying next to biceps and triceps that satisfied my fleshly desires. Quite contrary to that fact, I feel more vulnerable than anyone. In order for me to fulfill the task that lies ahead, *I must tell my story and still fight to remain clean!*

∞

THE DEVIL IS NOT A RESPECTER OF PERSONS. IF TEMPTATION MADE ITS WAY TO JESUS, THEN, GUESS WHAT? TEMPTATION WILL "STRAIGHT DISS" YOUR TITLE, YOUR GIFTS, AND CALLING!

∞

Spirit Versus Flesh

We've experienced enough flesh in this decade to last throughout eternity. We come together and trade hollow stories that are just shells of the truth. Looking for answers, we dance and jump and have an emotional high only to return to our separate bondage when the meeting is over. Too often, we go home neither challenged nor changed.

We must understand that the Bible says that we are not debtors to the flesh. We don't owe the flesh anything. The flesh can't compensate your spirit. The flesh and the spirit are not in cooperation, but they are in competition. The following is a Scripture that supports that statement:

For the flesh lusteth against the Spirit, and the Spirit against the flesh: and these are contrary the one to the other: so that ye cannot do the things that ye would (Galatians 5:17).

For too long we've depended on the flesh to do what only the Spirit can do. People have tried to deliver you from your flesh while working in the flesh. If I would allow it, my flesh would supersede my spirit, making me hold back on what I need to say. The Scripture says that my flesh desires to do anything that my spirit does not want to do. The apostle Paul wrote that these two are contrary to one another. That means if my flesh says yes, my spirit says no.

I must be honest with you: my flesh tells me not to proceed because I'm uncomfortable with some of the things I have to say, but my spirit compels me to go on. I asked the Lord, "Why must I reveal *my* secrets?"

He told me that His people have heard enough junk. They have heard enough Bible stories that tickle their ears, but still allow them to live comfortably while doing fleshly things. I sense very strongly that the Lord is fed up with people being comfortable in their lustful ways while no one addresses the issues.

∞

THE LORD IS FED UP WITH PEOPLE
BEING COMFORTABLE IN THEIR
LUSTFUL WAYS.

∞

The only person who can adequately address these issues is someone who has experienced them. When God places a mandate on your life, He will lead you to do risky things—things that make you feel uncomfortable and vulnerable—so understand that if He doesn't walk you through the process, you will miserably fail.

Without the Lord to govern the things I do and say, I am a hopeless case. I am totally dependent on His Lordship in my life. Announcing that He is Lord of my life automatically makes me subject to scrutiny in all areas. That's why the awesome task of uncovering myself is so difficult. My flesh said, "What if you fail? What if, after the book or CD, you fall?" If that happens, then I guess I'll have to listen to my own CD and read my own book. Ha! Ha! Ha! I would have the same opportunity as you, and that is to experience the power of the message *No More Sheets*.

Entering Into Covenant

I feel as though I am about to enter into covenant with many of you who have longed for someone with whom to share their innermost thoughts. But, in order to enter into true covenant, I must do as Jonathan did with David. These two men sealed one of the most powerful covenant relationships found in Scripture.

> *Then Jonathan and David made a covenant, because he loved him as his own soul. And Jonathan stripped himself of the robe that was upon him, and gave it to David, and his garments, even to his sword, and to his bow, and to his girdle* (1 Samuel 18:3-4).

My heart is heavy with the burdens of people who hide their secrets and suffer behind fake smiles. I have such a deep love for God's people, and I want to see them live victorious lives. This is why I must strip myself as Jonathan did. As painful and embarrassing as it may be, I have to take off my garments to show you that I am vulnerable too. I am willing to uncover myself to cover you.

❧

MANY PEOPLE HIDE THEIR SECRETS
AND SUFFER BEHIND FAKE SMILES.

❧

I must do as many ministers should and put away the sword of condemnation that all too often wounds our own warriors. When Jonathan gave his sword to David, he was saying, "If you ever feel a sword to your neck, it will not be mine. I will never bring you harm. I surrender to you today everything I have that could hurt you. My motives are to help you and not harm you."

Jonathan also gave David his girdle, which was what he wore closest to his body. He was saying, "I will divulge even the things closest to me to prove my commitment to you. Even those things which are attached to my loins I will give to you because of my love for you."

That's what I am saying to you. I will take those things that are close to my heart and give them to you. I am only here to help you. I am willing to be wounded to heal your wounds, because I…really…love…you!

The Vulnerability of Nakedness

Christians often forget that we are not on a playground, but a battleground. The Lord told us to prepare for warfare. Entrenched in the very idea of war is an understanding that there will be some wounds. This is a very important lesson: We must learn to survive the wounds. Believe me, I understand the scars that come in the heat of battle.

Even as I write, I must fight the groans of my flesh that tell me to pull down the shades. Why? My hesitancy reveals an important issue in the Body: We are so afraid of someone taking advantage of our nakedness that we keep ourselves totally covered. Whether mine or yours, wounds will not heal without getting some air.

❧

IN ORDER TO BE FREE, WE MUST
REMOVE THE MASKS. NO LONGER
CAN WE COMFORTABLY ENGAGE
IN BEHAVIOR THAT WE KNOW IS
UNGODLY.

❧

Why must I become open to be healed? Because my bandage hinders my healing. Uncovering a wound accelerates the healing process. I am not suggesting that you tell your husband, wife, or friends about your issues, but I am suggesting that you use my exposure to adjust your own experience.

I understand that people may violate you at your most vulnerable moment. Sometimes even those closest to you will take advantage of you. They appear to be coming to your rescue while contemplating your demise. In order for me to really open up, I must risk the possibility of even my closest friends or family members taking my secrets and trying to use them against me.

But do you know what I love about God? He gives us examples of what we're going through to let us know that someone else has gone through it, too. Noah's son took advantage of his father's nakedness. Look at what happened to him:

> And Noah began to be an husbandman, and he planted a vineyard: and he drank of the wine, and was drunken; and he was uncovered within his tent. And Ham, the father of Canaan, saw the nakedness of his father, and told his two brethren without (Genesis 9:20-22).

During Noah's most vulnerable time, his own flesh and blood took advantage of him. Having become drunk, Noah was temporarily out of control—just like some of us who have slipped into situations and done things we later regretted.

The Bible says that Noah was drunken, which is symbolic of his being overcome by the flesh. He needed someone's help to regain his composure. Instead of Ham seeing the need of his father to be covered, he took advantage of his vulnerability.

This is what many of us do in the Body of Christ. We act like crabs and try to pull each other down. We kick our wounded brothers and sisters. Like Ham, we tell our brothers about someone else's misfortune.

In the meantime, a group of people in the world cry out, "How do I come out of what I am in?" They need to see people who have gone through what they have been through and survived to tell about it. The Lord told me that I would have to be bold enough to risk my reputation to set the captives free. It's not easy to open yourself to criticism. But I'm dependent on God, and I know that He will vindicate me.

With that thought in mind, I release myself to the Lord to use me in any way that He deems appropriate. If I offend you, bear with me. If I insult you, tolerate me. If I embarrass you, understand me. But I have to take you through the process of purification. I must use the anointing on my life to liberate you at all cost.

I have a mandate from Heaven to solidify singles so they may find satisfaction in a Savior. I must divulge some truths to the divorced so they can reach their divine destination. I also must challenge the couples so they can be more than conquerors in Christ. Finally, I must offer hope to a dying world so that they can have all that God has promised them.

How will I do this? By exposing myself to ridicule. By opening myself to rebuke and by unveiling myself for persecution. With the help of the Lord, I am going to untie the sheets that have been attached to so many and unleash a new battle cry against promiscuity, adultery, pornography, and incest and help you declare that there will be no more sheets!

∞

Unleash your battle cry against promiscuity, adultery, pornography, and incest by declaring that there will be *NO MORE SHEETS!*

∞

CHAPTER TWO

The Voice of Experience

One of the most prolific teachers of our time is experience. It is very difficult for me to listen to someone explain the route to a place that he has never been to. But if he's been there, he knows the landmarks and the road signs. He can tell me where I need to turn. Should I expect delays because of construction? If he's gone that route, he knows. His experience tells me things I can't find on any map.

If a person has never seen a strawberry, she can't tell me what a strawberry looks, feels, or tastes like. The person could not describe the coarse outer texture that sends a certain sensation to the tongue. She can't tell me that the meat inside is smooth and gives an interesting contrast to the coarse outer layers. Being able to describe a strawberry indicates that a person has actually experienced this fruit.

When I hear someone clearly speaking in a particular area, I know this person has experience in that area. Many wrong and ridiculous anecdotes circulate around the Church world; they bring more confusion than lasting change. This is especially true in the singles arena.

I have heard many messages on how to cope with, confront, or conquer being single. Many of these talks would have carried greater weight if the speaker wasn't going home to his spouse while I returned to the lonely confines of my home.

Wouldn't you like to hear "Hold on!" from someone who's holding on themselves? If that married speaker rolls over in the sheets with their mate, they don't understand the ache in my heart. If they indulge in back-rubs from their mate, they can't fathom my longing to be touched.

I know what it's like to taste bitter tears in the middle of the night, just wishing someone was there to hold me. I know what it's like to believe God for a prayer that seems like it will never be answered. I know what it feels like to wonder if my time will ever come. Only a person who has experienced my pain can tell me that they know how I feel.

∞

IF YOU ARE LIKE ME, YOU WANT TO
HEAR, "HOLD ON!" FROM SOMEONE
WHO IS REALLY HOLDING ON.

∞

Truth Be Told

Listen, I've been in several unhealthy relationships. They weren't good for me—and I knew it—but I was dull of hearing. All I wanted was a relationship. My mouth was saying the right things, but my body was doing the wrong things. I have been there, and I know what I am talking about.

Some people are already thinking, "How can she say these things?" I refuse to be a hypocrite. Some people think that because I am Prophetess Juanita Bynum, the Lord has taken away my physical desires. Let me inform those people that they are wrong! You haven't heard enough people tell the truth. Everyone wants to sugarcoat it and say, "Bless God, the Lord is keeping me." Well, maybe He is, but sometimes He is keeping me in spite of my own feelings.

My flesh is not exempt from temptation. Even as the Lord speaks in one ear, the enemy screams in the other ear. The days of the three-step plan for overcoming your enemy are over. I know what I am talking about because I have tried just about everything to be free.

∞

YOUR FLESH IS NEVER EXEMPT FROM TEMPTATION.

∞

I have been in services where a preacher told me to write a former boyfriend's name on a piece of paper, crumble the paper, and then throw it over my shoulder while telling the devil that it's over. After all that, the same problem was still sticking to me like my skin.

I was told to stand and spin around three times and tell the devil that I was spinning out of it. When I got through spinning, I was still in the same web, but spun even tighter.

I know somebody just slapped your hand to your mouth and said, "I know she didn't say that." Yes, I did. Some of you want me to give you a bunch of hallelujahs and praise the Lords and tell you that I'm just running for Jesus and haven't gotten tired yet. I am not going to perpetrate a lie. I get tired many times, but

His Word strengthens me every day! That's right. The process is one day at a time. I wrestle every day of my life to walk in the integrity of the Word.

Yes, I am Prophetess Juanita Bynum, but I am not dead. I know you think that you cannot be anointed and still have a desire to sleep with someone. Some think that because I am anointed, I never get frustrated. They think that I never want to have some serious sex. They think that I don't ever want to do something wrong. Let me tell you that the devil is a liar. If you're telling that lie, then you're a liar, too.

∞

EVERY DAY OF YOUR LIFE, YOU MUST STRUGGLE TO KILL THE FLESH.

∞

Every single day of my life, I struggle to crucify my flesh. If you told the truth, you would say the same thing. I know what it feels like to go to the mall or the laundromat and see fine men everywhere I turn. Sometimes I wish I wasn't a prophetess. I think, "I wish I could give this man my cell number or my office phone number. No one has to know. I will do this just one time. I can get away with it." But we know that's not true.

Let's Be Honest

Some of us refuse to be honest, but God has directed me to snatch off some covers. For too long we have hid behind what we are *supposed* to be instead of being who we really are. The Bible never said you wouldn't be tempted. Superman is dead. Will some of the real Clark Kents please stand up?

∽

FOR TOO LONG, WE HAVE HID
BEHIND WHAT WE ARE SUPPOSED
TO BE INSTEAD OF BEING WHO WE
REALLY ARE. SUPERMAN IS DEAD.
WILL SOME OF THE REAL CLARK
KENTS PLEASE STAND UP?

∽

Do you know what's wrong with so many of us today? We won't be honest. If we're not honest, we won't be free either. I am sick of people lying to me. I am sick of people telling me that they have no problems. We have too many preachers in the pulpit who act like they got everything together. That very lie is carrying many people to hell because no one feels they can live up to the standards of the people of God.

I'm writing to reveal the secrets of the cloth. Listen to me: The bishops have struggles. The pastors have struggles. The prophets have struggles. Most of us are afraid to tell you, but the heat is on everywhere—maybe not in the area of sex, but there are faults, bloopers, and blunders in all of us who are called to ministry.

Why must I tell it? I must tell it because there are too many sheets hanging in the pastor's study. God wants to heal us, but we must be honest first.

∽

DON'T EVEN PRETEND LIKE YOU'RE
PETER PAN OR TINKERBELL IN THE
BODY OF CHRIST—SO STRONG IN
EVERY AREA AND FLYING SO HIGH IN
THE SPIRIT THAT YOUR FEET NEVER
TOUCH THE GROUND.

∽

The apostle Paul told the Ephesians to put away lying and speak truth to each other. If we're members of each other, then we need to be honest. The truth is, we get tempted—sometimes more than we want others to know! The passage in its entirety states:

Wherefore putting away lying, speak every man truth with his neighbour: for we are members one of another (Ephesians 4:25).

Just because you're standing today does not mean that you might not fall tomorrow. Paul told everyone to be on guard. The very second that you drop your guard, you may as well expect a hit. That very thought implies that we are vulnerable. He did not distinguish vulnerability by position. Just like King David could fall, so can we!

❧

JUST BECAUSE YOU ARE STANDING
TODAY, THAT DOESN'T MEAN THAT
YOU MIGHT NOT FALL TOMORROW.
THE SECOND YOU DROP YOUR
GUARD, EXPECT A HIT.

❧

Understanding our vulnerability, let's look at a passage from First Corinthians:

Wherefore let him that thinketh he standeth take heed lest he fall. There hath no temptation taken you but such as is common to man: but God is faithful, who will not suffer you to be tempted above that ye are able; but will with the temptation also make a way to escape, that ye may be able to bear it (1 Corinthians 10:12-13).

Verse 13 says that all temptations are common. Let's make one thing clear: Temptations are not wrong. Yielding to a temptation is wrong. Many Christians have been deceived by the devil into thinking that just because they want to do it, they may as well go ahead and do it. If we did not want to do it, it would not be a temptation.

∞

THE DEVIL TRICKS US INTO THINKING THAT JUST BECAUSE WE WANT TO DO SOMETHING, WE MAY AS WELL GO AHEAD AND DO IT.

∞

Temptation is designed to test your resistance. It doesn't mean that you automatically fail just because you were given the test. The teacher must grade your answers before he determines whether you pass or fail.

Many of us think that when the enemy hands us the test, we have failed. That is not true. Your grade is determined by how you answer the questions on the test. This is what's wrong with many of us in ministry—we see our name on the test and become bewildered. We didn't think we should have been given a test at all; consequently, we don't tell the world that we had a test. We want everyone to believe we are exempt, but that's a lie.

Sheets don't discriminate. They will try to wrap up any body. Sometimes this starts early in life. Believe me, I know. Let's journey back to the beginning so that you can understand my story.

∞

TEMPTATION IS DESIGNED TO TEST
YOUR RESISTANCE. IT DOESN'T MEAN
THAT YOU AUTOMATICALLY FAIL JUST
BECAUSE YOU WERE GIVEN THE TEST.

∞

My Early Years

I must begin by making this announcement: You have not been whipped until you have been whipped by *my* parents. I remember one time my mother told me that if I was going to call the police on her for abuse, then I had better go ahead and call because she was going to jail that day. My parents were trying to rescue me from sheets then, but it just did not sink in.

Before I go further, please understand this: People don't just wake up one day in the sheets. There is a process in, and there is a process out. It's just like going through a maze. Once you've hit a dead end, you must retrace your steps to get out. If I start at the beginning, you'll better understand the process of getting in and getting out.

∞

YOU DON'T JUST WAKE UP ONE DAY
IN THE SHEETS. THERE IS A PROCESS
IN AND A PROCESS *OUT*.

∞

When we were growing up, society was different than it is today. Today people call discipline spankings and time-out. But when I was coming up in the "villa of color," we got "killings"

56

and "stompings." There was no such thing as a time-out. We got *knocked* out. Whatever you did, you remembered it and vowed never to do it again. If you are from the "villa of color," you know exactly what I mean. Whatever you did to get the killing, you have never forgotten it. If you got whipped for stealing, after that whipping, the new law was *Thou shalt steal no more*. A lot of things are different now, but we even got whipped for not cleaning the kitchen right.

Let me tell you about cleaning the kitchen. We didn't just wash dishes like the kids do now. In my house, cleaning the kitchen meant mopping the floor, wiping in and outside of the stove, cabinets, and refrigerator. We had to take out the garbage and clean the can. If we didn't complete the job, it didn't matter how late it was, Mother woke us up. Jolted out of our sleep by a mad woman towering over us, we panicked. We wondered if this was a demon or our mother. (Mothers don't look like themselves when they are upset in the "villa of color.")

My parents were and are very loving people, but they believed in discipline. My father used to give us the famous "Scripture whipping." If he told us something two or three times, yet we disobeyed repeatedly, he discerned that a spirit was driving us. He put the Word of God on us. My father pulled up a chair and told me to sit down. He then told me what the Lord was saying while interjecting a hit with the belt about every ten minutes. He told me, "We're not going to run. We're not going to sweat this one out. We are going to hear what the Lord has to say." Have you ever had a whipping take two hours? I have.

We were trained to clean and cook. Today we call it chores for which we receive an allowance. Back then, we did not know what an allowance was. For cleaning and cooking, we were "allowed" to sleep in our parents' house. We were "allowed" to eat their food and drink their water. We were also "allowed" to take a bath, and that was the only "allowance" we knew.

We went to church seven days a week. There was no such thing as "I don't feel good." The kids across the street went to the doctor when they got sick. We got blessed oil on our head and fervent prayer.

One time, my mother told us to be on the front porch before the street lights came on. I stayed in the park and tried to beat the street light home because we lived on the corner. Wrong! That evening after the street lights came on, I saw a shadow coming down the street in house shoes with a belt in hand. I could hear the belt saying, "Come across the street, 'cause I got somethin' for you." That was only the beginning. At that moment, that's when all the kids in the park became a choir of angelic voices that sang, "Oooooh, here come your momma, and you getting ready to get a whipping!"

Despite my being daring and mischievous, I sensed a prophetic anointing on my life even as a teenager. Scripture tells us that God can place His calling on our lives at an early age. Look at the prophet Jeremiah:

> *Before I formed thee in the belly I knew thee; and before thou camest forth out of the womb I sanctified thee, and I ordained thee a prophet unto the nations* (Jeremiah 1:5).

Whatever God has called you to be, you were born with that gift. In order to be used of God, the gift in you has to be purged. I had not set myself apart for the Lord's purposes. My prophetic anointing was evident in its early stages, but I flowed in ignorance and made ignorant decisions. This was especially true in the area of relationships.

❦

THE SPIRIT OF TRUTH LIVING IN YOU CAN STAND UP TO *ANY* SEDUCING SPIRIT.

❦

Where My Sheets Began

My sexuality awakened during my teen years. This was the time when we started sneaking and kissing and touching in the basement, while the saints were upstairs in the meeting having church. We were fondling each other and passing out phone numbers. My parents taught me the sanctified way of the facts of life. The devil allows us to receive the correct method while trying it out another way.

This is where iniquity begins. Iniquity is doing a thing without God in it, doing it illegally or doing it the wrong way. My parents taught us about sex education the legal way, but the flesh wanted it through iniquity. That is very important in understanding how you get wrapped up in your sheets.

❦

INIQUITY IS DOING A THING THE WRONG WAY, ILLEGALLY, AND WITHOUT GOD IN IT.

❦

After this, I did something that was critical in my journey down the wrong road. I was the daring one in my family—the ringleader. I bought a pornographic magazine called *Black and White Love* and brought it into my parents' home. Every now and then, when Mother left the house, my sisters and I

59

got the magazine and discussed the pictures. This magazine was filled with men and women having what the saints called inordinate sex.

We secretly looked at these pictures as often as we could. Harmless as we thought it was, that stuff got into our spirits. Remember now: my parents were Holy Ghost-filled and sanctified people, but the spirit of pornography had already begun to wake up that appetite for sex outside of God within us kids.

❦

PORNOGRAPHY IS NOT HARMLESS.
IT GETS INTO YOUR SPIRIT AND
AWAKENS YOUR APPETITE TO
FORNICATE.

❦

We did not get anything over on my parents though. My mother, who is a very spiritual person, discovered our secret. I came home one day, and my mother was sitting at the kitchen table drinking coffee. When I headed toward my room, I noticed that everything was torn up with the mattresses overturned. Later I called this the "famous moment."

I was a little confused about what was going on, but I noticed that sitting there on the table in front of my mother was the magazine. She just calmly drank her coffee and read her Bible while waiting for me to come home. I knew that day that we would die a great death! In the "villa of color," when your parents are infuriated, they don't beat clothes. Mother said to us, "Since you want to be naked, strip off all them clothes. I ain't whipping no clothes, because I pay too much money for them." That was one beating I shall never forget!

Some years passed, and I reached the tender age of 19. I was in love with someone at school, but we broke up. That was my first heartbreak. Many of us don't heal from heartbreaks like everybody else does. Instead of allowing someone to process us through the healing, we think that time heals. Many times, time does not heal; that hurt seeps into the crevices of our spirit. As we go through relationship after relationship, hurts pile up in our spirits, and we can handle only so much. If you've never dealt with years of accumulated pain, watch out! If it surfaces all at once, you could be in some serious trouble. Do you see the connection? The only thing that a spirit of pornography wants to do is attach itself to hurt so that the insensitivity to the Law of God can begin.

❧

YOU ARE AT WAR AGAINST THE
ENEMY OF YOUR SOUL. UNTIL THE
DAY YOU TAKE ON IMMORTALITY,
THERE ARE NO PEACE TREATIES
WHERE THE DEVIL IS CONCERNED.

❧

Another Sheet

Have you ever met somebody and decided in your heart that this is it? The two of you agree to meet somewhere within the next few days. During that time, however, the other person meets someone else and things don't develop.

That's what happened to me in 1978. I met a guy who I felt was very wonderful. He was someone I felt could really make me happy. But, he could not decide between another girl and me. My self-esteem was so low that I was willing to accept mere crumbs from the relationship. I didn't feel that I was deserving of all of this man's life—just a part of it. When you allow a situation like this, a man will give you just enough to keep you hooked, but not enough to say, "I do."

❦

SEDUCING SPIRITS USUALLY ATTACH
THEMSELVES TO PEOPLE WHO, FOR
SOME REASON OR ANOTHER, SUFFER FROM
LOW SELF-ESTEEM.

❦

A mutual friend called one night to say, "Juanita, you're a beautiful woman, and you don't have to settle for this. He's not as committed to you as you think he is."

"I don't believe that," I told her.

"Hold on the phone line while I call him. Don't say anything—just listen."

What did I hear?

"Yeah, I think Juanita is nice," he told my friend. "She's a very beautiful woman, but I'm leaning toward this other woman. I'm not going to tell Juanita my decision just yet."

❦

WHEN SEARCHING FOR LOVE IN ALL
THE WRONG PLACES, YOU'LL FIND
ONLY MASKS HIDING
DECEITFUL FACES.

❦

When I heard that, it devastated me. I lived with the expectation that perhaps he would leave this other girl and come to me. When it didn't happen, I felt very rejected. I buried that hurt and started looking for love in all the wrong places. During this period, I met my husband. Whew, let me breathe a moment.

When my husband came along, he was not God's will for my life. He carried baggage that had traumatized him years before. Despite all of these unresolved issues, the trick was the fact that he said and did things that I wanted my previous boyfriend to say and do. I began to daydream, putting him in the place of the man I really wanted. Does that sound like some of you?

∞

YOU'RE NOT A CHEAP THRILL.
YOUR PURPOSE MUST BE FULFILLED;
THEREFORE, STAY STILL UNTIL YOU
KNOW GOD'S PERFECT WILL.

∞

This fantasy blinded me. I wasn't looking for purification in him. I didn't check his character for integrity. I didn't even consider his relationship with his parents or anyone else. He was attractive, and he gave me a ring—just what I wanted the other man to buy me.

Do you know what I did? I created my own fantasy in my heart and mind. I bought a number of magazines on weddings. I focused on beautiful dresses, limousines, and dinners. The whole relationship had all the telltale signs of a wonderful wedding, but not a happy marriage. Let me tell you, there's a major difference between the two!

I remember standing in the doorway of the church before walking down the aisle. I turned to my father and said, "I am making the biggest mistake of my life." My father told me that he would go down the aisle and tell the preacher that I had changed my mind if I wanted him to. I looked around at the limos, decorations, and crowd, and thought about the big reception, the tall cake, and my gown and decided to go through with it. I realize now that this was the beginning of my sheets *and a great big trick!* That was one of those times I played myself.

∞

IF YOU WANT A DIAMOND RING AND A BEAUTIFUL WHITE DRESS, BUY THEM FOR YOURSELF AND WEAR THEM TO THE NEXT CHURCH BANQUET. DON'T LET THEM BE YOUR MOTIVATION FOR GETTING MARRIED.

∞

Becoming One Flesh

When I got married in 1981, I was a virgin. Giving your virginity to a person affects you in a powerful way. When there's a separation, you never really get over it. The person can be a low-down, dirty dog, but something in your stomach always jumps when he is around.

When you haven't allowed God to purify you, and you meet another individual who is impure, the pull from the enemy overcomes you. The joining of those two people becomes a stronghold in the spirit realm, just as it would be if you joined yourself to God. It's not the will of God for your life, but it becomes a soul tie.

∞

STRONGHOLDS ARE THOUGHTS, CONTENTIONS, BELIEFS, TRADITIONS, AND LEGALISTIC RULES THE DEVIL SETS UP IN OUR MINDS.

∞

The Bible says that a husband and wife are joined together and become one flesh. Our wedding was wonderful, and we consummated the marriage. Three months later, I said, "Oh my God, what have I done?" Marriage vows are powerful. They go to levels that we really don't understand. Way back when I was looking at pornography, I was entering into that bond illegally. The Bible says that marriage is honorable and the bed is undefiled.

> *Marriage is honourable in all, and the bed undefiled: but whoremongers and adulterers God will judge* (Hebrews 13:4).

When you enter into that bond illegally, and then marry someone who is not the will of God for your life, you have to be prepared for the consequences.

Marriage requires commitment, but pornography doesn't teach you that. Centerfolds don't teach you to focus on the emotional and spiritual side of the person you've become attached to. Pornography focuses on genitals—not the whole person—and glorifies a physical sensation. That dirty book or video never tells you that you have just joined your soul to someone else's soul.

❧

WE'RE TO REPLACE WORLDLY IDEOLOGIES, CONCEPTS, AND PHILOSOPHIES WITH THE PRINCIPLES OF THE KINGDOM AND WORD OF GOD.

❧

Approaching sex outside of God creates its own blanket of residue on you. Do you know what the results are? You'll find yourself attracted to people who are not purged, just like you. These people are not the mates God intended for you.

We say that we just "clicked." We have "chemistry." No, what you have is the same perverted spirit. You have the same unclean nature, and spirits attract their own kind. This is how you end up with someone who you think is for you. However, when you go through the process of purification, you will see that he's far from the right person. The difference will blow your mind.

That's why people who are considering marriage must seek godly counsel. Many people say that they will make it because they just love each other. You may think you're in love, but you just may be after sex, and sex doesn't need true love to operate. Sex will take care of itself.

The question is, "Have you been processed to compatibility? When you don't feel like having sex, are you still close? What happens when you don't feel like going in the sheets? Are you flexible with the way you relate to your husband? Is he your brother? Is he your friend? Can you go to the zoo with him?" He's got to be somebody you can laugh with and share with. Why? Because sex is not all there is to marriage.

When touching, handling, and fondling enter your relationship, it distorts your focus on the spirit of the person. Instead, your attention is drawn to their flesh. You begin to desire each other's genitals more than you begin to desire to see the Spirit of God in each other. You can always tell when it's that kind of relationship because when there is no sex, you don't have anything to talk about.

You find yourself doing stuff out of the ordinary to satisfy your nature and his. That can become annoying, especially when your mind is preoccupied with something else.

Lovemaking starts on your feet. If you call from work and tell me what I mean to you and come home with flowers, that's when lovemaking begins. Lovemaking starts when you wake up in the morning. It starts when you help with the kids. It starts when you call during the day to see how I am doing. It starts with ministering to my spirit.

When two people join themselves sexually, it's not just a physical act. Their spirits are really joined together as one. Why? Because when you are at work, you are concerned about the other part of your body at home. While walking into the grocery store, you think about what your mate wants to eat. That is what it really means to be one.

∽

ACCORDING TO THE SPIRIT REALM,
YOU BECOME ONE WITH EACH
PERSON WITH WHOM YOU HAVE SEX.

∽

Looking Back

When I married, I wasn't thinking about any of that. I was clueless. I didn't consider ministering to the man. I didn't think about what he had been through. I didn't concern myself with staying on my knees to press him to another level in God. I was too young and immature to understand the power of carrying the weight of someone else's life. When everyone told me that our problems weren't my fault, I accepted that as the truth.

It wasn't so much as the wrong done to me—he was just being himself. You have to research his background enough to realize what you're getting. But remember this: you promised to love and cherish. You vowed to protect and minister to him. It was a lie. Don't blame anyone else. You just lied. Many of us don't want to admit it, but that's what really happened. We did not know the real weight of those words.

This starts us down the road to the sheets. We feel comfortable when we can blame the other person. Deep down, we know that it's really our fault, too.

When you realize that you could not keep your vows, it makes you angry. You went into the situation with the wrong motives. You had big ideas for the wedding, but not a clue about marriage.

Have you ever noticed what happens at a wedding? Everyone walks down the aisle slowly, but go out of a wedding quickly. Maybe somebody needs to change that tradition. Let's create a new one where you have to walk out of the church as slowly as you walked in. I think people have the concept that they can come into the marriage slowly, but they can get out quickly.

Looking back, I should have prayed more about God's choice of a husband for me. It's such a major life decision. Do you know that the proper method to receive anything from God is by prayer and supplication? Read this:

> *Be careful for nothing; but in every thing by prayer and supplication with thanksgiving let your requests be made known unto God* (Philippians 4:6).

∞

THE PROPER METHOD TO RECEIVE ANYTHING FROM GOD IS THROUGH PRAYER AND SUPPLICATION.

∞

If your mate has not come through prayer and supplication, then you have chosen that mate illegally. Your relationship has a shaky foundation. Only deep repentance by both parties can repair the damage. If you date and marry in the flesh, I can tell you this: expect extra, extra, extra problems along with the problems that marriage already comes with.

That's exactly what happened to me. My husband and I had additional conflicts in our marriage that we couldn't resolve. I had no idea that the next several years would take me through hell on earth.

∞

PRAYER IS THE FIRST STEP IN SUBMITTING TO GOD.

∞

CHAPTER THREE

My Shattered Life

When my husband and I moved to Michigan, I was ministering and preaching. But when cracks appeared early in our marriage, I felt the tension between my public ministry and private life. As the fault lines spread, major upheaval was inevitable.

Not being one to tell my business to everyone, I kept quiet and tried to deal with it on my own. Eventually, I confided in my pastors. By that time, our problems had grown to earthquake proportions. Feeling trapped in a bad marriage, the enemy tempted me with desperate thoughts—thoughts that I fought hard to control.

Wanting to End It All

One night while visiting my pastors, I felt an overwhelming urge to kill myself. At that moment, it seemed like the right thing to do. I didn't have enough strength to say, "I can't do this to myself." I couldn't take any more, but I didn't have the guts to walk out of the marriage. I felt that the easiest solution was to end my life.

I swallowed every pill in the medicine cabinet. Then, I walked out of the bathroom and said, "I'm tired and I'm going home." Since I only lived a few blocks away, they didn't think anything of it.

After I left, however, God prompted my pastor's wife to check the bathroom. Seeing the empty pill bottle, she told her husband what I had done. They jumped into their car. When my pastor saw me, he lunged into the street just as I was crossing the intersection. An 18-wheeler truck was upon us. My pastor snatched me, and within seconds the truck ran over my empty shoes.

God spared my life because He had a purpose for me. He wants me to tell you that you can overcome the pain. You can make it. You can tell the devil, "There will be no more sheets!"

∞

DON'T GIVE UP. IF I CAN MAKE IT, YOU CAN MAKE IT!

∞

At the hospital, my stomach was pumped. I awakened saying, "I don't want to live. I don't want to live." What was my problem? I was in a bad marriage, but the Holy Spirit wouldn't let me leave. He kept telling me, "You can't go yet. You can't go yet." I said, "God, how much more can I take?"

∞

BELIEVE ME, I UNDERSTAND WHEN YOUR SOUL CRIES OUT, "I CAN'T TAKE IT ANYMORE. I MUST BE SET FREE NOW. IT'S AN EMERGENCY!"

∞

Fulfilling My Vows

I finally realized that I needed to ask the Lord to forgive me for not consulting Him. I started to pray and get before the Lord while listening for an answer. The Lord told me that the only thing that would bring healing to me was to fulfill my vows. Everything that I had declared at the altar had to be fulfilled in order for me to be free. Now that's heavy.

The Holy Spirit spoke to me and said, "I will get you out of this. But when it's over, you're going to come out blameless. I don't want anyone to be able to say that you were wrong. I want you to come out with the testimony that you did what you were supposed to do—you kept your vows."

∞

ALL OF THE VOWS YOU MADE
TO GOD AT THE ALTAR MUST BE
FULFILLED IN ORDER FOR YOU TO BE
COMPLETELY FREE.

∞

That's when I made sure my floors were clean enough that he could eat off them. I began cooking his dinner. It did not matter what the relationship was like—I had vowed to do my part. I did what I knew a wife should do. I walked in repentance and lived up to the words I had spoken before God, our families and friends, and each other.

Despite my efforts, we separated. One day, my husband came to the church and told me during a service, "It's time for me to go." He gave me the keys to the house, and he left. His decision stunned me.

Embarrassed by being abandoned, I felt like a failure. I was raised to believe that if your marriage failed, something was wrong with your womanhood. Back then, older women taught that you don't run out of a marriage. You stay there and work it out.

When you get married, another life comes into your life. When that person leaves, a death occurs and mourning begins. Everything of his that's not a part of your character—or a part of the character of God—has to be torn out of you. It's a painful process.

I didn't have the emotional strength to deal with the problems in our marriage. Neither did I have the strength to deal with the fact that I was being abandoned, especially after working so hard on my character as a wife. *I was devastated!*

∽

BELOVED, I DON'T CARE IF YOU
HAVE FAILED A THOUSAND
TIMES—*KEEP GETTING UP AGAIN!*

∽

Welfare Woes

While married in the early 1980s, I had worked three jobs. Racked with emotional pain from the separation, I couldn't work anymore. Unable to cope with life, I went on welfare.

Things got so bad for me until one of the church mothers took me to the Goodwill store to get boots because my old ones were falling apart. This was a luxury for me since, in the past, I had to pay two dollars for my winter coat and 50 cents for my boots.

As a matter of fact, my mind goes back to the building where I collected my food stamps. It was so small that we often lined up outside. While standing in that line, wearing a two-dollar coat from the early 1960s, I thought, "Why am I out here? God, my life is not supposed to be going this way!"

The Lord said, "I'm birthing purpose in you. I've got to take you this route. I need you to stop complaining. I need you to yield your will to Me. I've got to take you through a breaking."

∞

LORD, LET YOUR WILL BE DONE IN MY LIFE.

∞

Many times, I didn't have money or food. One day I was sitting in my cold house—my gas had been turned off. Why didn't I ask for help? God made me shut my mouth. I couldn't ask anyone for anything. God wanted to be Jehovah Jireh—which means my Provider. Not many days later, God began to prove Himself to me.

A sister walked up to me and put five dollars in my hand. I began to leap within my heart from the excitement of finally having some money. Boy, it felt good to be able to have five whole dollars to myself. As I entered the church service that night, I went in giving praise and thanks to God, knowing that the Lord had heard my prayers. But that night, something strange began to happen. The Lord led my pastor to take a second offering that evening. I gave two of the five dollars that the sister had given me. In my mind, I planned to buy myself something to eat with the remaining three dollars.

Then the pastor said, "We need three more dollars."

I thought, "I don't think so!" *(smile)*

75

The Lord said to me, "Give the three dollars."

I resisted until the Lord repeated, *"Give the three dollars!"*

As I left service that night feeling very despondent and very empty, I wondered within myself, "Didn't I just have five dollars in my hand when I walked into the church, hungry? Now I'm walking out of the church broke again." While walking down the street, thinking hard about that money, I heard a voice shout, "Sister Bynum, the pastor wants to see you." I turned and heard the shuffling of feet and realized it was a deacon in our church. When I got back to the office, Pastor said, "Sister Bynum, I don't know what your need is, but the Lord told me to raise this offering for you." He handed me nearly $500! That would turn on my gas, pay my telephone bill, and buy groceries. Boy, did I feel stupid; the very offering that I struggled to give was being raised for me!

Do you know why Prophetess Bynum always gives in offerings? Because when I was in debt, God began to teach me to give my way out of desperate situations. I learned to lean, depend on, and trust God. He has never failed me.

❦

IF YOU CAN'T GIVE GOD YOUR MONEY, IT WILL BE HARDER TO GIVE HIM YOUR LIFE. SINGLES OUGHT TO BE THE BIGGEST GIVERS IN THE CHURCH.

❦

Bad Decisions

Because of the problems in my marriage, I watched my whole ministry unravel. It was very difficult to know that the most intimate details of the breakup of my marriage were floating around my church. Even now, some things are too painful to share. By not allowing others to help me and by not being honest, I cut myself off from God's grace. Pride forced me to handle this crisis myself.

I thought to myself, *I should have gone to college and done something productive. Instead, I fed my spirit the wrong things. I also spent time with the wrong people. Their comments influenced my attitudes toward marriage and men. Instead of listening to my pastor, I listened to them.*

❦

ASK THE LORD TO REMOVE FROM
YOU PEOPLE WHO SUBTRACT FROM
YOUR LIFE AND REPLACE THEM WITH
PEOPLE WHO ADD TO YOUR LIFE.

❦

Listen: If you embrace the carnal side of things, you'll get carnal results. But if you feed on the Word, you can have great peace no matter what your circumstances. Some of my closest friends are going through divorces. Because I constantly feed them the Word, they have been experiencing life and peace to such a degree that they're amazed at the way they're handling things. You always think about what you should've done when you were in a mess!

❦

THE ONLY PERSON WHO CAN
ENCOURAGE YOU TO KEEP MOVING
TOWARD DELIVERANCE IS SOMEONE
WHO HAS THE SAME GOAL.
THEREFORE, WATCH THE COMPANY
YOU KEEP.

❦

You see, during the breakup of my marriage, my friends at the time did not do that for me, but I can't blame them for my actions. Instead of dwelling on the Word of God, I allowed myself to be consumed with negative emotions, and it had devastating consequences. You may not see it now, but anything that God allows there's a reason for it and it will be revealed, you just wait and see!

Nervous Breakdown

By 1983, I began to internalize my feelings and fell into fear, dread, and self-pity. One evening, I blacked out. The last thing I remember is getting up from the dinner table. One of the deacons of the church found me walking down the middle of the boulevard without shoes. It was snowing outside, and I was wearing only a T-shirt and jeans. I had literally lost my mind!

I remember going to the hospital. The doctor said, "Whatever is wrong with this girl is locked inside her. Her mind is gone, and she will never be right." I sat in a padded room and banged my head against the wall repeatedly. I was dead on the inside. I couldn't even talk. You know what? I can't really explain to you what I felt. Despite the voices I heard in my head, I knew God had a purpose for my life. Even though I didn't know how to get out, I knew that I would come out of it. I just didn't know how!

∞

YIELD YOURSELF TO *His* TREATMENT
AND ANALYSIS.

∞

One afternoon, my parents paid someone to drive me from the hospital in Michigan back to Chicago. A trip that should have taken 4 hours took 13 hours because I kept jumping out of the car. I told the driver, "Stop the car! I can't breathe." When I got out, I started to run. They chased me into the trees and the enemy thought he had me; he thought that I would never be right!

When I got home that Sunday, my mother helped me to get dressed for church. As we drove there, I was talking to myself out loud. After church, we pulled in front of my parents' home. When I got out of the car, the sky went black. The enemy whispered, "The rapture has already taken place. You're left behind!" I fell in the yard and started screaming.

For days I lay naked in my mother's bed. I couldn't stand for any clothes to touch me. My mother had to lock me in her room, where I laid screaming every now and then. I remember my mother lying down by my bed and praying.

One night I heard her say, "God, You said that You would use her for Your glory."

I remember grunting with a deep sigh of relief. It was comforting to know that in the middle of my turmoil, somebody was praying for me—and, to make it better, it was my mom.

Regaining a Sound Mind

Two nights later, as I laid there very somber in my spirit, I had a vision in which the ceiling opened up. Two hands came from the sky and tied one end of a string onto one mountain and the other end onto another mountain. Then the hands put me on the string between the two mountains.

I heard the voice of the Lord call out saying, "Come to Me, Juanita." I took several steps. Then all of a sudden, I began to lose my balance because I looked down. There was fire all under me.

I was in fright of what I saw. The voice said, "Keep your eyes on Me, and as long as you do that, you will never fall."

I began to walk toward this voice, which I knew belonged to God. Then He said, "Let this mind be in you which is also in Christ Jesus." When He said that, I sat up in bed and began to speak in tongues. The Holy Spirit communed with me for two hours. That's when I saw myself preaching before thousands of people. When I came out of the spirit realm, I grabbed the blanket, put it around me, and ran through the house saying, "I'm healed! God has healed me!"

The Lord miraculously broke a spirit of insanity from my mind. God began to tell me, "A mighty deliverance will come to My people because of your testimony."

I'm prophesying to you right now:

You're not going to have a breakdown. God is going to give you a breakthrough. The devil won't take you out. He won't wreak havoc in your life. The enemy knows there's a deliverance ministry inside you. He knows you've been equipped with a purpose—to bring people out of bondage. Whatever you're going through, you will make it. You're coming out with a sound mind.

Right now, tell yourself and the devil, "I'm coming out of this—and I'm coming out with my mind filled with the wisdom of God. I shall not die but live and declare the glory of God. No weapon formed against me shall prosper. The Spirit of the Lord is lifting up a standard against the enemy."

❧

WHEN YOU SAY, "LORD, HELP ME,"
THE SPIRIT TAKES THE WORD AND
LIFTS UP A STANDARD AGAINST
THE DEVIL.

❧

What the devil meant for your harm, God is turning it around for your good. Right now, lift up your hands and begin to praise God! You have to put your entire being—even all the hurt that you're feeling—into worship. You must bring yourself into worship. What the enemy has lodged in the secret places of your mind can't stay.

You're not going through this alone. I've been there. Whatever you're feeling, I've felt it, too. That's why you see me on the platform praising God with my whole heart. People say, "She sweats too much; she preaches too loud; she's always hollering; she's always jumping; she's always falling out."

Do you know what I say to those people? "You don't know where I've been. You don't know what it took to get me to my place in God!"

∽

BEING ALONE IS NOT THE SAME AS
BEING LONELY.

∽

A Double Deliverance

Do you think the devil stopped there? After God restored my mind, my body suddenly went haywire. Two years after I was delivered from the spirit of insanity, I struggled with anorexia nervosa. That was in 1985.

My stomach wouldn't accept food. Even the sight of it made me sick. Soon, I couldn't even imagine myself eating. My clothing went from size 16 down to size 5. My weight dropped to 114 pounds. I was so skinny that my shoulders stuck out. I hadn't been that small since I was a child. I was depressed and

I began to pine away. My mother had to cook food and make me eat it. She sat there and prayed with me that the food would go down.

Don't ask me why I signed up for college. I only got halfway through the semester. Because of not eating, I couldn't even function and had to drop out of school. At the time, that was the only way I thought I could deal with my problems.

That may have been my most pressing issue, but it wasn't my only spiritual problem. I also had an attitude toward Caucasian people. God used an interesting scenario to defeat both of these enemies on the same night.

I wanted to visit a church that I saw on television, so I asked a girlfriend to take me there. The church seated over 6,000 people, but only a few dozen African Americans were in the service. While listening to the man of God, I said, "God, I need a miracle. If You don't heal me completely, I'm not going to make it."

As I responded to the pastor's altar call and went forward for prayer, God prompted a Caucasian sister to walk from the choir and stand directly in front of me. She began to prophesy, "The Lord spoke to me and said that you're a woman of God who is chosen by Him. Greatness is locked in your loins. God told me to come over here and break the spirit of anorexia nervosa off of you." And she shouted down in my ear, "I command you to live!"

When she laid hands on me, I hit the floor. When I got up, I was instantly healed. After the service, I went to a soul food restaurant and ate my first full meal. God had healed me! At the same time, God delivered me from a nasty spirit of prejudice.

While getting rid of sheets, you don't know who has your deliverance. You don't know where it's coming from. You don't know who God will use. I am prophesying to you: God is not going to leave you in the state that you're in. There is a victory for you. You need to open your mouth and say it right now: "There is a victory for me and God; I want it. It doesn't matter who brings it; I just want to be free."

∞

GOD IS NOT GOING TO LEAVE YOU IN THE STATE YOU'RE IN. VICTORY IS YOURS!

∞

What About Your Husband?

Some of you might be saying, "You've certainly been through a lot! What about your husband? What did he do to you? What kind of man was he to cause you such pain?"

God has given me a platform to speak to the Body of Christ. It's very easy to forget about those people who don't have a platform. It is easy to take that power and misuse it by telling my whole story. Exploiting my ex-husband does not make me a better person. Talking about him doesn't make me more than I really am. That is not necessary.

I could say, "Well, he did this and he did that. Oh, honey, let me tell you some things about him." But that's not what caused my relationship or my mind to go bad. What I *allowed* in my life put me in those situations.

I was already messed up when I got married. I already had low self-esteem, and I already had issues with my character that were not resolved. There was no discipline in my life.

By the grace of God, I yielded to His discipline. That's when He began to refine me. Scripture says:

> *But He knoweth the way that I take: when He hath tried me, I shall come forth as gold* (Job 23:10).

I could have said, "I can't stand men because of all that I've been through. I hate my husband. Because of him, I had to endure welfare, anorexia nervosa, and a nervous breakdown." But you don't get healed that way. I had to admit that those things happened because I didn't know the Bible. I wasn't full of the Word of God. I didn't have wisdom to avoid those snares. I heard a preacher say that bitterness has a porcupine effect on your inner man. When you harbor bitterness, it gets in your belly and tears you up. You don't destroy anyone but yourself.

❧

BITTERNESS DOESN'T DESTROY
ANYBODY BUT THE ONE WHO
IS BITTER.

❧

Look in the Mirror

You need to explore what it is about you that may not be right; do this before you dwell on what was not right in your mate. You can't change your mate, you can only change you. That's why I had to forgive my ex-husband.

As you read about all the relationships I went through, ask yourself: "Who had the problem?" Although my ex-husband had some problems, you will see that I had problems too. I kept falling into bad relationships. By the way, let me remind you that even after him I continued to make bad choices. That says that the problem didn't start with him; it started with me!

✜

STOP BLAMING OTHERS. YOU NEED
TO EXPLORE WHAT IT IS ABOUT YOU
THAT MAY NOT BE RIGHT.

✜

When you make marriage vows and don't fulfill them, a lot happens. You disappoint God, your spouse, and yourself. You get caught in a negative cycle of blame, guilt, and regret. This leads to self-pity. This spirit says, "I'm nothing. I'm worthless. I'll never be anything." Eventually, the spirit of your mind will regulate you to a level where you don't belong. While you are debased, low-life people become attracted to you.

That's the beginning mind-set of your sheets. Why? Because you feel you have to go to bed with someone to prove your womanhood or manhood, and sometimes that means anybody; therein lays the problem. We feel that being a good man or woman is defined by what we do in the bedroom. Quite to the contrary, being a good person is defined by what you can do for my spirit.

Sexuality in marriage is God's way of adding life to your life. When you marry for the wrong reason, life is added to death, which produces nothing but death and destruction in your spirit and emotions. Nothing will work out.

Sex may be wonderful, but the enemy uses that to give you an illusion that your marriage is great when really it is not. One day you'll wake up and look in the mirror. Your eyes, which are the windows of your soul, can't hide the truth. You'll say to yourself, "I'm a dead woman. I'm a dead man. I've had good sex, but my spirit is dead."

If you are planning to get married soon, please ask yourself some questions. What is your level of process? Where are you in your level of purification? What damage are you about to do? Whose soul are you about to kill?

If you're not serving God, you're serving the devil—there is no middle ground. If you've joined yourself to the devil, you've joined yourself with death. That death may be slow, but it is inevitable.

∾

THE OPPOSITE OF GOD IS THE
DEVIL—THERE IS NO IN-BETWEEN.

∾

My Divorce Becomes Final

When my marriage ended, I did not rush to judgment. I waited almost three years before I was divorced. I did not want to use divorce as a cop-out to neglect my responsibility. Knowing that God's perfect will for marriage was not divorce, I left open the door to reconciliation. Only after my husband decided that he no longer wanted the marriage, and with godly guidance from my pastor for over two years, I filed for divorce. My pastor prayed over me and said that the time was right to make the move.

I will never forget the day that my pastor's wife went with me to court. I thought, *Well, it's almost over.* When the judge's gavel came down and he pronounced my divorce final, I could not get off the stand. I could not move. My attorney looked at me and said, "Ms. Bynum, you can step down."

Immediately the tears began to flow. A cry erupted from my soul. I could not get up from that seat. I went through a death in that courtroom. My pastor's wife had to help me out of the building. For three days, I cried and cried, but I really did not understand why.

Then the Holy Spirit told me, "Don't you know that another person lived inside you, and he just died? Your spirit was just divided from your soul mate."

∞

BROKEN PROMISES FROM THOSE YOU
HAVE BEEN WITH WILL STEAL A PIECE
OF YOUR SOUL.

∞

It was horrible. Divorce is painful. I couldn't hold it together. The failure beats your brains out. If you truly want to make things right, you won't look at the other party and talk about what he did and did not do; you'll begin to analyze yourself. When you see so much wrong in yourself, you can't even bear it.

∞

LET GO OF YOUR PAST AND
YOUR FAILURES.

∞

I'm telling you my story to let you know that weddings never last; true ministry does. Marriage really is ministry, and it's deeper than the excitement of a gown, limousine, and gifts. Wedding fantasies are not the foundation for a strong marriage. If you build on those superficial images, they will destroy your life.

When I got divorced, I asked the judge for my name back. A few years earlier, I hadn't realized the significance of taking on someone's name. Scripture puts a high priority on having a good name.

A good name is rather to be chosen than great riches, and loving favour rather than silver and gold (Proverbs 22:1).

When you accept a man's marriage proposal, you take his name. That name carries whatever is in his lineage, including generational curses. He will become the covering for your life. If you're single, don't be so quick to give up your name, just for a sexual high. That's a price I don't think you want to pay.

A Long Detour

Someone might say that my ministry seems as if it has shot up overnight. Well, in some ways it did. God had to push me forth in a hurry because I was so late and behind schedule.

Pit stops in the sheets are like putting a recorder on pause. You get out of the sheets and repent, someone hits play again. By the time you really get moving, you meet another man. Before you know it, you're back in the sheets. You hit the pause button a second time. After doing this for so many years, you've lost a lot of ground. Once you've finally realized what has happened, you're in your mid-thirties and way behind schedule. When you repent, God, in His mercy and purpose for your life, has to rush the process to put you back on schedule.

∞

GOD CAN TURN YOUR EVERY
MISTAKE INTO A MINISTRY AND
A TESTIMONY.

∞

I believe that's why everything for Juanita Bynum has flourished at one time. I made so many unnecessary stops before I got it right. But isn't it good to know that when God has a plan for your life, He gets you to your destination? I don't care what kind of seeds the devil plants; when God has a plan for your life, He uses even your sheets to lead you to victory. He will turn every mistake into a ministry and then into a testimony.

To this day, I can testify that my ex-husband and I are friends. He has remarried. We were able to discuss our relationship in a manner that revealed what was wrong with us individually before we got married. We pinpointed the things in us that contributed to our bad marriage.

If you've made a mistake, it doesn't mean that life is over. God redeems even the worst situations. The apostle Paul, once a persecutor of the Church, understood the richness of God's grace:

> *Moreover the law entered, that the offence might abound. But where sin abounded, grace did much more abound...* (Romans 5:20).

That grace is still available today, and it's available for you.

❈

JUST BECAUSE YOU MADE A MISTAKE, IT DOESN'T MEAN THAT LIFE IS OVER. YOU CAN CONQUER YOUR SHEETS!

❈

Don't Dance With Delilah!

In light of the fact that I've battled my way out of the sheets, I can now show you how to conquer yours. You are going to recognize the warning signs. The next time someone puts his arm around you and wants to kiss you, you'll realize that it is not just a kiss—it's danger! It's a dangerous dance with Delilah. Let me show you what I'm talking about:

> *And when Delilah saw that he had told her all his heart, she sent and called for the lords of the Philistines, saying, Come up this once, for he hath shewed me all his heart. Then the lords of the Philistines came up unto her, and brought money in their hand. And she made him sleep upon her knees; and she called for a man, and she caused him to shave off the seven locks of his head; and she began to afflict him, and his strength went from him. And she said, The Philistines be upon thee, Samson. And he awoke out of his sleep, and said, I will go out as at other times before, and shake myself. And he wist not that the Lord was departed from him. But the Philistines took him, and put out his eyes, and brought him down to Gaza, and bound him with fetters of brass; and he did grind in the prison house* (Judges 16:18-21).

Delilah wasn't after the secret to Samson's strength; she wanted his vision. Samson refused to recognize the caution signs all along his highway to disaster. The Spirit of God eventually departed from him. God had to use the loss of his eyesight to turn him around.

∞

RECOGNIZE AND HEED THE CAUTION SIGNS THAT LEAD TO YOUR HIGHWAY TO DISASTER.

∞

Samson had a calling from God, but he lived out of his carnal nature. Because he broke the Nazarite vows that were upon him from birth, he went sailing right into sin and bondage to his enemies. When he cried out, God strengthened him one last time. There is a deeper revelation to this that my dear brothers will encounter in a later chapter.

If you are a long way from God and have fallen into immorality like Samson, today you can call on God in repentance, receive His forgiveness, and begin the restoration. God wants to give you strength and vision for your life. But if you dance with Delilah, God's best will remain out of sight—and out of reach.

Are you still hesitant to come out of those sheets? Let me share with you how I got ensnared in unhealthy relationships. If you see yourself, take heart; God has made a way of escape. If God can deliver me, I know He can deliver you.

∽

DON'T WAIT UNTIL TOMORROW...
COME OUT OF THE SHEETS TODAY.

∽

CHAPTER FOUR

How Did I Get Wrapped Up?

L et me go back a little bit. About two weeks after my divorce, I got ready to go out. As I stood in front of the mirror, it dawned on me: "Oh my God, I'm single again." It was a strange feeling. Although it wasn't the best marriage, having a husband offered a sense of security. I felt I belonged with someone. Suddenly, I became fresh meat at the market.

I wasn't ready to date again. I needed a lot of emotional healing. I didn't understand it at the time, but now I know that when my husband left me, it was a sheet.

∞

HAVE THE COURAGE TO SAY,
"LORD, UNTIL YOU ARE FINISHED
PROCESSING ME, PLEASE DON'T SEND
ANYONE MY WAY."

∞

Let me explain. Remember, sheets are layers of emotional baggage that you get through sexual experiences. Even though we had a legal marriage, when he left me, it was a sheet. Something happens when you get a divorce. You don't trust yourself or your judgment anymore. The last time you said, "I do," you made a mistake. You ask yourself, "What if I make another mistake?"

Being single again was a horrifying experience. I don't know how everyone else reacts to their divorce, but my eating spun out of control. Boy, was I a wreck. My figure ballooned from a size 9/10 to a size 16. During that period, my clothes became lethal weapons. My skirts were cutting off my circulation, and my turtlenecks from when I was skinny began to suffocate me. I began to be killed by my own wardrobe. I allowed my self-esteem to hit rock bottom, instead of allowing God to help me deal with the divorce. This was doubly bad. I became vulnerable to anyone who showed me any attention.

I desired another relationship. It really didn't matter that the person was not in the will of God for my life. I just wanted to date someone and wanted somebody to say to me that I was not ugly or a throwaway.

∞

ASK THE LORD WHAT HAPPENED
IN YOUR PAST TO MAKE YOU
VULNERABLE PRESENTLY. ASK THE
LORD; HE WILL ANSWER YOU.

∞

An Unequal Yoke

One of my first relationships really angered my pastor. I went out with someone who wasn't saved. Desperate for love, I was open to the devil's deception. I thought, "Well, I really don't care if he's not saved. It really doesn't matter that he's not a Christian, as long as he treats me nice." That only made a bad situation worse.

∽

DESPERATE FOR LOVE, MANY
COMPROMISE BY THINKING, "AS
LONG AS HE TREATS ME NICE, I
REALLY DON'T CARE IF HE'S SAVED."

∽

The Lord had me under the strict tutelage of my pastor, which was good because I needed some accountability. My pastor gave me some ground rules that were not optional, but mandatory.

"Juanita, you don't need to sing in the choir or usher. You don't need to do anything for about a year except sit down and be healed. Allow yourself to be ministered to and take the Word of God into your spirit."

He told me I needed to allow the Lord to heal my emotional trauma. "What emotional trauma?" I asked myself. I didn't even recognize how badly I was wounded. I had no idea my actions revealed the underlying devastation. I felt that crying for the first couple of days was enough. Wrong!

∽

ALLOW THE LORD TO HEAL YOUR
BROKEN HEART.

∽

If you are going to "throw a sheet," it will take more than a couple of days of tears. Instead of expressing my grief, I held everything in. I dealt with the pain in my own way, but my hurt began to spill over and affect areas of my character.

I started going out to dinner with a man who was not saved. My pastor heard about the incident and questioned me after church one Thursday night.

"Where did you go last Saturday night?"

Surprised that he knew, I hesitated. (That's when you want to pretend that you don't even speak English.)

"Juanita, where were you?" He pressed the issue.

There's one thing about me that you must know: I tell the truth. That is one quality my parents raised me with that I really appreciate. I did not and do not like lying. Pastor knew that I would tell him the truth about anything he asked me.

"I went out to dinner."

"With whom?"

When I mentioned the man's name, I knew Pastor was disappointed. It had been two years since the divorce, and I was singing in the choir. Seeing me on the verge of another emotional disaster, my pastor was loving, but firm.

"Juanita, I can't let you sing in the choir while you date an unsaved man. And no, you can't direct the choir, either. I want you to sit down for a while. I'm putting you on a sabbatical. I want to see you on the front row for every church service. You need to sever that relationship. It's just your flesh crying out."

His wife agreed and, reluctantly, so did I. "That's not the way you resolve hurt by adding more hurt to it," he said.

So what did I do? I sat. Oh boy, did I sit. I thought I would rot on the pew. Though I was sitting up straight, my insides looked like a desert man hanging off the side of the pew, with my tongue slurped out of my mouth crying desperately, "Water! Water! Anybody help me." I sat so long and so hard that my skirt and my slip were stuck to my thighs. Now that's some long sitting. (Ha! Ha!)

∾

DON'T BE AFRAID TO CRY OUT TO YOUR DADDY. THE LORD WON'T REJECT YOU.

∾

Excuses, Excuses!

Every time I turned around, I was messing up again. My pastor and others kept saying, "See, here you go again." I just want to tell you all that I had some real issues—I mean some 'ish'-shoes' with Nike's and Rollerblades on. My pastor began to sound like a broken record. I can still hear these words, "You missed Bible study Tuesday night. You weren't at church Thursday night, and you came late Sunday morning. Something is wrong. You told me that you ate something and were too sleepy to come back to church on Sunday night."

Do any of these excuses sound familiar to you? My excuses were so weak. I told my pastor that stuff, not knowing he had passed my house after church. All the lights were on and my boyfriend's car was parked outside. Sheets will make you dumb, too. I could've had him park around the corner, but you know where my mind was. I was trying to get my groove on.

Do you know why I was like that? Because I missed my feeding. You see, a real doctor will examine a sick, underfed baby and tell someone to get an IV started immediately. After the child begins to regain strength, the doctor will then order the parents or nurse to put the child on a strict diet. They get the child some food because he is malnourished. Yes, the parent may have been feeding the child, but if the diet consisted of a lot of junk, the child didn't receive enough nutrients. The IV will supply the child with the right vitamins and minerals. Like a negligent parent, I did not feed my spirit the right things. I was too weak to fight off the illness.

∞

WHEN YOU START FEEDING YOURSELF THE WORD OF GOD, YOU CAN HANDLE ANY TEST THE DEVIL SENDS YOUR WAY.

∞

My pastor told me that I was going to keep traveling around the same mountain until I decided to get my feeding. I didn't even notice that every time I went around, I was being filled with another spirit. I was making my deliverance difficult because I was piling on more sheets. The sad part was I did not see anything wrong at the time.

I didn't have sex with some of the guys I dated, but the passion between us during the fondling stirred such an appetite. It was so strong that I wondered what they would be like. The pursuit of the feeling was almost like a "high."

∞

FONDLING IS NOT INNOCENT. IT IGNITES YOUR DESIRE TO HAVE SEX.

∞

I will tell you this: I am saved and filled with the Holy Spirit. I don't care how saved you are, wrong times and places will mess up your mind. Because I had a problem with submission to authority and I was not in church—which was the right place for me to be—I saw my pastor as a preacher and not as my lifeline. I saw church as a place where I greeted my friends and not as a place to receive my feeding. You don't join a church because the pastor has cute hair, Versace suits, nice eyes, or any feature like that. The question is this: can his Word ministry and the level of his anointing give you life?

∞

IT DOESN'T MATTER HOW SAVED YOU ARE—BEING IN THE WRONG PLACES AT THE WRONG TIMES IS JUST WRONG.

∞

The Shock of My Life

I would like to start by recalling a particular relationship. While I was engaged to a guy, I visited a girlfriend one evening. She smiled and told me how proud she was of the way I was handling this guy's recent marriage. I glared at her and said, "What did you say?" She covered her mouth and asked, "Didn't you know?" Imagine my finding out that a guy I *thought* I was about to marry, had already married someone else. I fell off her barstool.

Do you want evidence that going to church is not enough? I didn't meditate on the Scripture I had just heard preached in church. Many people hear the Word, come home, and never pick up the Bible again until the next service. Do you know that you're supposed to go home, take the same passage that your pastor preached, and research it?

My reaction to what my girlfriend said simply shows that I was going to church, but not eating properly. A real "Yes,

Lord!" was not in my soul. I was not agreeing with my pastor on that Word.

Do you know what I did? I bought the biggest bottle of whiskey I could find and got sloppy drunk. I was as drunk as five skunks.

Many of you have a hard time believing that. You ask, "Why would she do that?" That's a prime example of not having enough Word to sustain you during traumatic times.

A carnal person always resorts to fleshly solutions. Alcohol was the only thing that made me feel better for that moment; it's like temporary relief. Some people drink. Some smoke. Others do drugs. I was a babe in the Lord and had not obtained a high Word level. I had no Word in me to defend or fight for me. Now when I say babe, I had been saved for over seven years; but years don't equal maturity. You see, years without quality feeding only means wasted years.

∞

HOW OFTEN DO YOU TURN TO
GOD IN WORSHIP, PRAYER, AND
THE WORD? IF YOU'RE LIKE MANY
CHRISTIANS, YOU'RE MALNOURISHED.

∞

I vividly remember driving to the river bank, where I proceeded to drink and cry and drink and cry. I kept asking myself, "Why did it have to happen to me? Why do people always treat me like a dog?"

Finally I said, "Just forget it. I will drink this whiskey and jump into the water." Sobs welled up inside me all over again. I realized I would go to hell if I killed myself, which was not the thing to do. I decided to drive to my pastor's house instead.

I safely arrived at my pastors' house, but don't ask me how. I drove onto their front lawn and blew the horn. Pastor looked outside, and he and his wife came out and got me. I was crying and telling them how my friend had gotten married. I kept asking, "Why me?" I really wanted to die. I kept asking everybody if they had a gun and would they just kill me. You know, liquor will really make you talk crazy. They took me upstairs. That was the first time I had ever seen them weep for me.

When you're not flowing in obedience, your flesh and a man can pull you away from God's will. You don't just step out; you take a quantum leap away from God. That lets you know the whole situation was just a flesh party. You never even consulted God.

Listen: When something is born of the Spirit, the person always resorts to the Spirit for an answer. Likewise, when something is born of the flesh, a person always resorts to the flesh for an answer, tries to solve it himself, and just forgets about God.

"You Need to Be in Church!"

My pastor had sympathy for me, and I spent Saturday night at their home. After I woke up the next morning, the pastor's wife came in the room and asked, "How are you feeling today?"

"Really sick," I replied.

"That's too bad. But I have some clothes laid out for you, because you're going to church."

I was shocked! I thought, "Wait a minute! I have a hangover. I'm sick. I just lost my man. What do you mean, I gotta go to church?" She responded to my thoughts as if she heard them.

"Juanita, Pastor has seen where you have failed to conceive the Word. Now you really need to be in church. It's not that we don't sympathize with you, but you've broken a spiritual law, and you need to be restored. We want to help lead you into the presence of God, again."

There I was—a mental case with a busted kidney from drinking a whole bottle of whiskey—in church on a Sunday morning. Of course, the choir sang louder than ever. Oh, that was horrifying! The congregation praised God on with the volume turned to 10. That did my hangover a lot of good, huh?

That Sunday, pastor called me up for prayer, and Mother Margaret Hill came over. You don't know how her voice echoes in your ear when she's at the altar praying for you! I can hear her now praying for some desperate soul: "Give it to him! Give it to him!"

Every time she opened her mouth, my whole body vibrated. I didn't know whether I was going to throw up the alcohol, faint, or get totally delivered. I was in a state of confusion that day.

Hurting physically and emotionally, I began to weep at the altar. I didn't know why I was crying. Was it because I felt sick and wanted to throw up? Was it because I wanted to be saved? Maybe I was just plain delirious.

I fell to the floor and the room spun around. When they got ready to raise the offering, they had to pick me up off the floor with Mother Hill hitting me in my stomach and saying, "Tell the Lord, 'Yes!'" I thought, "God, I will tell You 'yes' all year if You will just not let her hit me again. I am about to barf all over this church!"

They sat me on the pew. My head tilted back, and slop ran out of my mouth. Terribly sick from the alcohol, I decided never to drink again.

I was sick for a few days. When the alcohol—and the sympathy—wore off, I still had a responsibility to deal with that sheet.

You can't make a legitimate, life-changing, permanent decision when sin is involved. If you do, you'll deal with the spirit of iniquity. Remember, iniquity is anything that you do without God in it. Basically, it's doing something using the wrong method or pursuing something illegally. It's not a scripturally sound decision.

∽

YOU *NEED* TO BE IN CHURCH.

∽

Eviction Notice

I was trying to get out of the sheets, but the task was very difficult. Do you know why? I had fed on self-pity for so long that it had become a ruling or chief spirit in my life. A spirit that strong won't just pack his bags and go. You have to forcibly evict him. You simply take your spiritual weapon, which is the Word of God that is sharper than any two-edged sword, and use it to tear down imaginations and every high thing that exalts itself against the knowledge of God (see 2 Cor. 10:5). The power of His Word is clearly stated in the Book of Hebrews:

For the word of God is quick, and powerful, and sharper than any two-edged sword, piercing even to the dividing asunder of soul and spirit, and of the joints and marrow, and is a discerner of the thoughts and intents of the heart (Hebrews 4:12).

Only the Word of God is sharp enough to cut that thing away from your soul without destroying you as a person. I began to apply the Word and got better for a while, but that's the trick. It's like penicillin; you take it until the symptoms of the cold are gone, but if you don't finish the prescription, the virus is not completely killed. In the midst of my feeding break, I met someone else out of God's will. Yes, you guessed it: there I went again.

Before I knew it, the fondling and kissing started again. Look at what I did: the ground that I had gained by using the sword of the Spirit was lost. I was defeated by my own flesh.

∞

IF YOU ARE NOT MARRIED—TO EACH OTHER—THEN DON'T TOUCH EACH OTHER.

∞

If I could use a medical analogy, it was as if lust was about to die in my life. But before the Holy Spirit could sign the death certificate, I met someone else and started kissing and touching. It was like giving that spirit CPR. My flesh said, "Stand back, everybody! We can't let this old friend die. Use every extreme measure to save him!" At that moment, his hands became suction cups; when he touched me, they sent an electric shock that revitalized that demon in my life. Before I knew it, I had picked up another sheet. Yes—and this one was worse than the last. What does the Scripture have to say about that?

When the unclean spirit is gone out of a man, he walketh through dry places, seeking rest, and findeth none. Then he saith I will return into my house from whence I came out; and when he is come, he findeth it empty, swept, and garnished. Then goeth he, and taketh with himself seven other spirits more wicked than himself, and they enter in and dwell there: and the last state of that man is worse than the first. Even so shall it be also unto this wicked generation (Matthew 12:43-45).

When that spirit is cast out, he eventually tries to come back. I'll tell you what happens. Picture this: The spirit is cast out. He and his buddies stand around wearing shades, smoking blunts, and drinking wine coolers, just waiting. They know that unless you fill that spot constantly with the Word of God, it's just a matter of time before they can send you another counterfeit and you will fall once again.

They even pause for a minute and ask each other, "You think we got a chance of getting back in there?"

One replies, "Just chill out man. She ain't got no Word. She ain't been to church in two weeks. She don't even like her pastor. She don't sing in the choir. She's empty. I'll whistle and give you the signal. It's just a matter of time, but we're going back in."

The enemy knows how you like your desserts. He knows what color you like. He knows which hairstyle appeals to you. He knows what kind of build will turn your head. Listen to me: the devil will definitely send you someone else.

Will You Wait for Your Portion?

When I thought I was delivered, I didn't have much money. I lived in the projects and everything around me was all messed up. I was in bad shape. The enemy kept enticing me to sin. While in those projects, I discovered that I was not strong enough to live by myself. My brother and sister came to live with me for a while.

105

Do you know why that didn't work? Being the oldest, I felt that I did not have any accountability to my younger siblings. Listen to this: One of the most important pieces to the process is having to answer to someone. I did not feel responsible to tell my siblings where I was going or when I was coming back. I knew I needed someone to answer to, so I moved in with Mother Lott, who was the church mother. All I can say is "Oh my God! Oh my God!"

Anyone who has ever lived with a church mother can concur with me and just say, "Oh my God!" Every single morning, I heard Mother Lott praying. Whenever she sensed I was about to do something, she spoke out of her spirit, "You gotta be careful. You gotta live like the rapture's coming right now. It's no time to be messing around. A lot of these men don't mean you no good. You have to live rapture-ready."

I had a problem waiting for God's man in God's timing. This Bible passage showed me that I wasn't the only one who wanted to have it all now.

> *To further illustrate the point, He told them this story: "A man had two sons. When the younger told his father, 'I want my share of your estate now, instead of waiting until you die!' his father agreed to divide his wealth between his sons. A few days later this younger son packed all his belongings and took a trip to a distant land, and there wasted all his money on parties and prostitutes. About the time his money was gone a great famine swept over the land, and he began to starve. He persuaded a heal farmer to hire him to feed his pigs. The boy became so hungry that even the pods he was feeding the swine looked good to him. And no one gave him anything"* (Luke 15:11-16 TLB).

Many people think the younger son asked his father for something wrong. That's not true. The son asked his father for something that he rightfully deserved, but it was not the right time. He said, "Give me my portion."

That's what happens to many singles. We ask God for our portion and feel that we deserve it. When God doesn't grant it to us in our timing, we go out and look for it ourselves. We try to get something illegally.

Like the prodigal son, we ask for "my portion," but not in "my season." The son didn't rightfully deserve his portion at that time. When I lived with Mother Lott, I was still looking for my portion, but it was the wrong time and the wrong season. Make sure that the season is ripe for apples when you go out looking to pick.

Blinded by Sheets

You can always tell when someone is in the sheets. These are some of the symptoms: that person will defy her parents, curse her sisters, throw her nose in the air, and defend herself to the last inch.

I know what I am talking about. You may say that you're not having sex. Even if no penetration has occurred, you've been aroused. That climax shuts down your ability to think clearly. Hormones are controlling you now—not your mind and definitely not your spirit. I know that's the truth. If you're honest, you know that's the truth, too.

We go into denial. The guy can be no good, but we say that he's so nice. We tell ourselves that no one understands him. No one else knows him like we do. We make excuses for him. We say something like, "His mother did him wrong and his father left him." Well, that's not your problem, but sheets make a person take on false burdens.

∽

THE FIRST STEP IS TO FIRST
ACKNOWLEDGE THAT THERE IS
A PROBLEM. WHEN YOU IGNORE
THE PROBLEM, YOU ONLY DECEIVE
YOURSELF.

∽

Sheets make you think you are "Zena" or "Wonder Woman" or "The Bionic Woman." You ooze with compassion for him when you've never had that much mercy for your own family. You find grace that even God has never seen. Believe me, sheets will also help you justify why you must have your needs met.

Sheets blind you to the obvious. You won't care whether he has a job or not. You won't even ask him when he last held a job. Sheets manipulate you to go out with him and pay the bill yourself. You even find yourself doing things in public that are a dead giveaway that you are in the sheets.

∽

THE SHEETS WILL BLIND YOU TO THE
TRUTH. ONCE YOU'RE SINGLE IN
HEART AND PURPOSE, IT'S AMAZING
WHAT YOU'LL SEE.

∽

What am I talking about?

When you have been in the sheets, your boyfriend can walk up behind you in the church lobby and put his arms around your waist. Neither you nor he thinks anything about it. That means nothing to you, but it's a dead giveaway to others. It means nothing to you because he's gone much farther with you behind closed doors.

That was my problem. I was just blind at the time. It did not matter what my pastor said to me. His words were like sounding brass and tinkling symbols. I was on a great mission. I had a mandate to fulfill, but it was not from God.

My pastor told me, "We've got to defeat this ruling spirit in your life. Until you come to grips with that, you will never be what God wants you to be. You really have to focus on that."

∞

IT IS YOUR DUTY TO FIGHT YOUR FLESH. IT IS YOUR DUTY TO WIN.

∞

Emotionally needy and embracing a "gold digger's" mentality, I stooped to all-time lows. To satisfy my flesh, I hurt people and embarrassed my parents. Low self-esteem makes you do things you thought you would never do. Looking back, I know that I was under the influence of a seducing spirit that was designed to take me out. You see, the Word of God says:

> *Now the Spirit speaketh expressly, that in the latter times some shall depart from the faith, giving heed to seducing spirits, and doctrines of devils; speaking lies in hypocrisy; having their conscience seared with a hot iron...* (1 Timothy 4:1-2).

∞

THOSE WHO EMBRACE A "GOLD-DIGGER" MENTALITY WILL STOOP TO ALL-TIME LOWS.

∞

Falling for an Older Man

While living in Michigan, I decided to go to Chicago for a weekend. I was living with the church mother and working a low-paying job, which reinforces an earlier point—I was very *needy*.

During this time, I met someone who I thought could help. This man was 28 years my senior, but I didn't care because he had more than I did. This is where many of us are deceived. When you have no direction, any road will do. When you have no money, anybody's paycheck will work for you.

∞

WHEN YOU HAVE NO DIRECTION,
ANY ROAD WILL DO.

∞

I remember that years before this relationship, I met a sister who went to church in the same city I lived in. We were not best friends, but we had a relationship. She had visited my house a couple of times, and we sang together. She had dated this particular man in the past. Some time had elapsed between her relationship and my meeting this man. It had been a long time since I had seen her, so I started dating this same man. He began to wine, dine, and buy things for me. I slowly but surely got strung out over all the attention and gifts. *Boy, was I blind!*

Believe me when I tell you that when you begin to walk in rebellion and disobedience and become disconnected from leadership, you are headed for big trouble. Back then, I was in an intense course called "Leadership Submission." It was not a class taught by our pastor. The Holy Spirit signed me up for His own personal training session. It was sometime after my divorce. I had gone through every step of my tutelage under my pastors. The Lord was getting to the core of my spirit. He really began to dig some things out of me that I was not aware were there.

❧

YOU MUST IDENTIFY WHY AND HOW YOU CAME TO BE IN YOUR CURRENT STATE. THEN YOU WILL BE BETTER ABLE TO APPLY AN EFFECTIVE, LONG-LASTING SOLUTION.

❧

Do you want to know one of the tricks of the enemy? While we're under training, things will happen in our relationship with leadership, and leadership will not always be correct. But, you have to realize that leaders are human beings, and they make mistakes. There is no perfect pastor. Pastors are in training by the Lord with every member who comes into their congregation.

At that time, giving leaders their proper place in my life was awkward for me. Because they had been there for so many devastating times in my life, I held them in high regard. Some situations occurred with several visitors to our church that really devastated me. I began to doubt whether or not my pastors were still really for me, but that was an illusion planted by the enemy.

Sometimes the Lord allows things to happen in your relationship with your leaders to test your ability to be led by the Spirit of the Lord in them. Regardless of the situation, you are not really walking in submission until you're doing something that you don't really want to do. I don't care what I see or what goes on or what I don't like. The lesson I learned from my first experience was this: did the Lord tell me to come to this particular body? The answer was *yes*.

∞

Your relationship with leadership tests your ability to be led by the Spirit of the Lord.

∞

When the negative situations began to occur, I had to ask myself again: did the Lord tell me to come here, and is God telling me to leave? My assistant pastor posed that question to me one day when I shared some things with him.

"If God is telling you to leave this particular church, you are released to go," he told me. "But if the Lord is not telling you to leave, you need to take the next step. Get before God and find out what's going on in the realm of the spirit. What is the enemy doing? What is God doing? What lesson is the Lord trying to teach you right now?"

I had to resolve those issues, but back then I was too immature to take the time to do that. Everything just got cloudy for me. They kept telling me, "Juanita, you need to be careful because the enemy has one trap after the next, but God has a plan for your life. The Lord has something for you, and you're going to be great in God." But during that time, I was suffering from rejection and not allowing God to heal me in the core of my spirit.

Pride is such a strong spirit. Even when we're hurt and wounded, we don't want to admit our pain. When going through a separation or divorce, we want to appear all right. We suck it up and say, "I'm going to make it anyway."

∞

PRIDE IS SUCH A STRONG SPIRIT
THAT IT DOESN'T ALLOW YOU TO
ADMIT WHEN YOU'RE HURT OR
FEELING REJECTED.

∞

The enemy saw how fragmented and fragile I was. He knew the only thing that prevented him from gaining a foothold in my life was my leadership. The shepherds of the Lord were there, and they were covering me. When the enemy sent a barrage of fiery arrows to take me out, my leaders protected me and undergirded me in prayer. They made it mandatory that I come to all-night prayer. It was mandatory that I fast and pray. They taught me how to make it through the trauma of my divorce, step by step.

Once again, though, the enemy devised a cunning plan to distract me. He used the power of dating someone older. As a single adult, I was somewhat embarrassed to lean on my mother and father. I didn't want to tell my business to my brothers and sisters. My pastors were only ten years older than I. The enemy laid the perfect snare for my feet. I fell into the older man/younger woman syndrome. This person *appeared* to have more wisdom and knowledge than my parents or my pastors. The lie from the devil is that he just appeared to know more. I thought I had found everything that I needed for emotional support, but boy, was I wrong.

Missing God's Timing

God has ordained a person to press you to the next level, and no one else can take that person's place. God has placed you in the womb of the Body of Christ. No one else can carry you.

113

You were in your mother's womb nine months for a purpose. Staying there for the full term ensured that your growth would be complete. That was your place of development, and that's what the Body of Christ is for you spiritually, especially the local body in which you have been placed.

When you accept Christ and God plants you in a body, it's like an artificial insemination. That body has been chosen to house you until you are mature enough to walk on your own. Stay there until you are mature enough to begin the ministry that God has called you to.

No premature baby has the right to walk out of his mother's womb. Even if he decides to walk out, he doesn't have the strength to stand. He can't see. He's totally helpless. He can't walk out before his time. He can't even do it when it is time. His mother's body works hard to push him down the birth canal and into the world.

The Body of Christ allows us to incubate, to grow, and to mature. That was where God had placed me, but the enemy wanted me to start my ministry prematurely. I had been in that one ministry for nine years. I was coming to my time of birthing—my time of delivery. I was almost on schedule. In my ninth month (I'm categorizing months as years), the enemy said to me, "You're ripe," but the power of delivery had not completely come. But I said to myself, "It's been nine years." The number nine is the month of delivery. So, I left. But I left because an evil influence beckoned me to come out before my time. I had not been birthed or pushed out in God's timing.

How do you know when you're walking against God? The timing doesn't agree with your parents. It doesn't agree with anyone around you. People who've been your friends for years suddenly don't know what they're talking about. That's when a chief spirit has seduced you. You're not ready, and the enemy is waiting to take you out.

Let a Shepherd Protect You

Submitting to authority shields us from the enemy's deception. That's why God placed pastors in the Body of Christ. The following passage describes the character of a shepherd:

> *The Lord is my shepherd; I shall not want. He maketh me to lie down in green pastures: He leadeth me beside the still waters. He restoreth my soul: He leadeth me in the paths of righteousness for His name's sake. Yea, though I walk through the valley of the shadow of death, I will fear no evil: for Thou art with me; Thy rod and Thy staff they comfort me. Thou preparest a table before me in the presence of mine enemies: Thou anointest my head with oil; my cup runneth over. Surely goodness and mercy shall follow me all the days of my life: and I will dwell in the house of the Lord for ever* (Psalms 23:1-6).

Why doesn't your girlfriend or boyfriend want to meet your pastor? A shepherd has vision that we don't have. A shepherd stands taller than we stand. He can see farther down the road than we can see. If the person you are dating is afraid to meet your pastor, he or she is not God's will for your life. Even now, when someone asks me out to dinner, I tell him, "You have to meet my pastor first."

Pastor may look at me with raised eyebrows and that tells me, "Get rid of him. He's not the one." Listen: women know women and men know men.

∞

IF YOU ARE AFRAID TO TAKE SOMEONE TO MEET YOUR LEADER OR PASTOR, THEN THAT PERSON IS NOT IN GOD'S WILL FOR YOUR LIFE.

∞

God placed leaders in our lives to watch over our souls. They are not against us. They are for us. That's why I would not advise anyone to date without seeking wise counsel about the person.

First ask yourself, "Why am I dating him? What need do I have that this person can fulfill?" If all your needs are financial or materialistic—these are blinders—that person cannot meet any spiritual needs. That person cannot pray you through. That person cannot encourage you to go to the next level in God. Has God sent him to help construct what He has already placed in your life, or has the devil sent him to destroy you?

∞

ASK YOURSELF: "WHY DO I WANT TO DATE THIS PERSON? WHAT NEED DO I HAVE THAT THIS PERSON CAN FULFILL? CAN HE OR SHE ENCOURAGE ME TO GO TO MY NEXT LEVEL IN GOD?"

∞

If you're needy, you're a prime target for the enemy. Look at what happened to me: Remember the older man who asked me to visit him one weekend? I left Michigan with no clothes or

116

anything and never returned. I just left. My sister had to pack all of my clothes and send them to me later. I told my pastor that I felt trapped and had to get out. I told him that it was just time for me to leave. That was the biggest mistake of my life.

After being in the relationship for some time, I discovered he was still dating the sister I mentioned before—the one I knew. My heart broke for her and me. Even with the pain, the enemy had me so tied into the relationship that I could not break it. That's how shrewd the enemy is—he will cause you to put a knife into your own sister's back for some sheets.

The enemy will send you someone who will meet your needs. Because I was so impoverished, anything he bought me looked too good to turn down. I started feeling like it was just this sister's loss and my gain. Sheets had stolen my sensitivity. Sheets had stolen my ability to be compassionate. They took away my integrity, my self-respect, and respect for others.

I know that when you repent, you can't go to everybody in your past. I believe some things are best left alone. But I feel that I must apologize to my sister because I believe we were both victims, not by the hands of just a man, but by the hands of a seducing spirit.

I Apologize

My dear sister in Christ, I caused you great pain. I know I said it before, but what I did warrants another apology. I am so sorry until I don't mind dethroning myself, in front of the nation, to say I love you dearly and I'm sorry. Please forgive me. I was blinded by sheets.

Dating Principles

How can you date someone whom your sister has dated? That's just not cool. Even before I got saved, I followed this principle: I never dated anyone my natural sister dated. In case you didn't know, it's taboo. I'm not speaking about your sister going out to dinner two or three times and discovering the guy wasn't her type. I have gone to dinner a few times and said, "I think my sister and you would be a better match."

But when you know or even think a sister may have been sexually involved with a man, don't date him. Or, if a sister has dated him for more than six months, then you two women need to talk. She must be allowed to say, "I see that you have an interest in this brother. We went out a couple of times. We both agreed that this is not the will of God for our lives. I don't want you to think that there is any emotional attachment between us." There is a right and wrong way to do everything.

When all three of you attend the same church, it feels weird. You need to have the integrity to say, "That was my sister's pain. I don't want to take my sister's pain and make it my joy." The enemy may deceive you and lead you to believe, "It didn't work out for them, but that's my man now." That's the way people in the street act. That is not the way for believers to conduct themselves with brothers and sisters.

You need to assist the man who is your brother in the Lord before dating him. Make sure that he walks in integrity. Has he left any scars behind? Has he wounded anybody? While you're testifying how the Lord blessed you with a husband, some sister may be bleeding because he emotionally and mentally abused her. If a sister in the Body of Christ has already dated a brother and you're interested in him, you must do some research. Whether you have a casual or close relationship with her, you need to talk. Asking a few questions could save you some big problems.

∽

RESEARCH YOUR DATES. MAKE
SURE THAT THEY ARE WALKING IN
INTEGRITY, HAVEN'T LEFT ANY SCARS
BEHIND, AND HAVEN'T WOUNDED
ANYONE.

∽

Now I want to talk to the brothers. You see, Proverbs says:

Whoso findeth a wife findeth a good thing, and obtaineth favour of the Lord (Proverbs 18:22).

That word *findeth* doesn't mean you try everyone then choose one of them. It means that you wait on the Lord.

When God shows you who your wife is, that's the one you choose—without leaving any damage behind. On your wedding day there should be a gathering of praise in the sanctuary. The host of witnesses ought to be able to say, "We believe in our spirits that this is of God." Do your family and friends have a witness in their spirits that God has orchestrated your marriage? Or, are five sisters sitting at home with pain and scars, remembering you were with them? They really feel sorry for the sister you're about to marry. Your brothers and sisters should be able to rejoice.

∽

BROTHERS, THE WORD *FINDETH*
DOESN'T MEAN YOU TRY EVERYONE
OUT AND CHOOSE ONE. WHEN HE
SHOWS YOU WHO YOUR WIFE IS, SHE'S
THE ONE YOU CHOOSE—WITHOUT
LEAVING ANY DAMAGE BEHIND.

∽

Women wonder, "What am I supposed to do while waiting for my husband to find me?" You're supposed to be obtaining the Lord's favor as well. Most of us know the above verse, but another Scripture also talks about gaining favor from God.

For whoso findeth me findeth life, and shall obtain favour of the Lord (Proverbs 8:35).

Sisters, you need to find God and get His favor on your life. How will your husband find you? He will recognize the Spirit of God in you.

∞

WHILE YOU'RE WAITING FOR YOUR HUSBAND TO FIND YOU, YOU'RE SUPPOSED TO BE OBTAINING THE LORD'S FAVOR. AS YOU FIND HIM, HIS FAVOR WILL SHINE ON YOU.

∞

The same God that he serves also lives in you. The same Spirit that leads him also directs your life. While you seek God, His favor will shine brightly on you. Honey, you'll be easy to find! Double favor resides in such a marriage. Then, the following Scripture will become a reality in your life:

The blessing of the Lord, it maketh rich, and He addeth no sorrow with it (Proverbs 10:22).

If you're not seeking God and His favor, you'll begin to stray. The enemy will cause you to look at your sister negatively as if she did something to cause the relationship not to work out.

You need to understand, when you are in the sheets, it really doesn't matter that she is your sister in Christ. You really don't know the true meaning of being sisters in Christ. We play sisterhood extremely cheap. Because of the blood of Jesus, sisters in Christ are actually stronger than naturally born siblings, but we need to realize that.

∞

INSTEAD OF BEING IN COMPETITION
FOR THE MEN IN OUR CHURCHES,
LET'S HELP EACH OTHER GET OUT—
AND STAY OUT—OF THE SHEETS.

∞

CHAPTER FIVE

Crawling Out of the Sheets

Remember the drama with the older man? Let me tell you what happened. I stayed in that relationship and did not call my pastor. Everything was crumbling all around me. When I finally contacted him, my pastor told me that they were on a serious consecration for me. He knew there was a purpose and direction for my life. He knew that the devil had sent a person to set me up.

While driving to work on the expressway, I heard the Spirit of God say, "It's over!" I began sobbing uncontrollably to the point that I had to get off the expressway and pull over to the side of the road! As those words echoed repeatedly, my stomach began to feel as if someone was ripping my insides out. It was as if His voice was amplified.

❧

GOD SAYS TO US, "MY CHILD, ALL
I HAVE WAITING FOR YOU IS LOVE,
LOVE, LOVE. COME BACK AND
EMBRACE YOUR PLACE IN
THE KINGDOM."

❧

I could not go in to work. While I sat in my car and cried, I turned the radio on to the Gospel station and at that moment, Joyce Meyers' radio broadcast came on the air. She taught about fighting against the will of God. Reverend Meyers explained that if you just trust God, He knows what He's doing; God has a greater plan than what you're trying to hold on to. I didn't want to hear that then! That was in 1988.

I had gotten a new car. I had clothes. I had jewelry. And, in spite of all I had received illegally, the Lord loved me so much! Listen, He began to warn me, show me, and speak to my heart. It was time for my deliverance to come. I know that if I had let go and obeyed God that day, I wouldn't have ended up in such bad shape.

What about you? Isn't it time to let God take over your life? He wants you to fulfill your unique purpose. You were born with a destiny. If you don't walk out, you will be devastated out. Either way, God will get you out.

※

YOU CANNOT GET WHAT GOD HAS
FOR YOU WHEN YOU'RE STUCK
BETWEEN THE SHEETS.

※

God sent me a word across the airwaves that day. He sent dreams and visions. I couldn't sleep at night because I was troubled. I dressed sharply and had a smile on my face, but I was being sucked into a black hole that just wouldn't release me.

"It's Over!"

Not long afterward, God sent me a word through my father. He asked me to take a trip with him out of town, which he had never done. I said to myself, "This is a setup!" We drove to a convention nine hours away. We had never traveled together alone. My father said, "I don't get into your business, you know that about me, right?" I said, "Yeah." He continued, "You haven't brought it up to me, but the Holy Spirit told me that this man is not going to marry you, and you are not to marry this man. God has a plan for your life. It's going to be awhile before you get married because God has a nationwide ministry for you."

The power of God was so heavy that my father had to pull over. He got out and walked around the car three times, while speaking in tongues. When he got back into the car, he was crying. Dad said, "The Lord just broke you free. Your deliverance just came."

I wept so much that when we arrived, I couldn't even go to the convention. We went to my hotel room instead. My father asked, "Are you going to the service tonight?"

"No, I'm not."

He said, "Your mind is still struggling with this word so I'll tell you this: The Lord told me to tell you to get dressed. Tonight, He's going to give you proof that this situation is over."

I still didn't want to hear it, but I got dressed. When I got to the service, I saw the man I was dating. When I walked up to him, he treated me as if he didn't even know me—as if we had just met. I didn't understand.

I went back to my hotel room. My father was looking all around the convention center, but he couldn't find me. Late that night, my father came to my room, knocked on the door, and asked me if I was sleep. "No, sir," I replied. When I opened the door, Dad saw my eyes. He asked, "You got your proof tonight, didn't you?" I said, "Yes, sir." I got in the bed and went to sleep. To tell the truth, I slept very deeply that night!

Surrendering My Will

A couple of months later, strange things started to happen. I knew that they were in the plan of God. One of the most peculiar and awesome things happened, and God began to reveal His great love for me.

I was so out of focus that I could hardly work. Arriving late, I just sat at my desk and stared into the distance. I felt my world was falling apart. Everything was going wrong.

My job performance had suffered so badly until one morning my supervisor called me to her desk. I feared the worst. She said, "We have to let you go."

I gathered my personal belongings and walked out in tears. When I got to the lobby downstairs, I called my mother.

"Momma, I just got fired. I'm depressed, and I don't know what to do. I don't know what's going on in my life."

My mother began to pray for me. "God's will is being done. He already told me that He's getting ready to do something else for you. You can't see it right now, but you need to praise God because He has a plan for your life. Just begin to praise and thank God."

On my way home, I stopped by my sister's workplace.

"I just got fired from my job," I announced.

"Let me see if my supervisor will allow me to leave," she said.

We went to a breakfast diner.

"I don't know what to do. How am I going to make it?"

She replied, "Juanita, take my keys and go to my apartment. Stay by yourself for awhile."

As I walked into her house, all I could say was, "Lord, I thank You."

Immediately, the Lord began to tell me, "I'm in control. I'm in control. I'm in control."

Sometimes, even now, when it gets rough in the ministry, I have to remember that God is in control. God is in control. Why don't you just say that right now, "God is in control!"

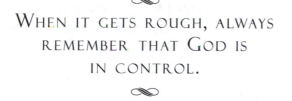

WHEN IT GETS ROUGH, ALWAYS REMEMBER THAT GOD IS IN CONTROL.

I remember telling the Lord, "God, let Your will be done. I'm tired. I'm at rock-bottom. I'm at the end of myself. I don't feel that my relationship with You is where it used to be."

I fell asleep, but got up around 2:00 P.M. to eat some cereal. Watch this: That same day, my sister-in-law went to my mother's house to pick up something. While there only briefly, the telephone rang. Pan American Airlines, who had my job application on file for a year, asked for me. She knew where I was, so she gave them my sister's number.

I was on my way out to the store when Pan Am offered me a job as a flight attendant. Can you believe that happened the very same day that I got fired—the very same day that I said, "God, let Your will be done"? I had always wanted to be a flight attendant. It was the job of my dreams.

After I was hired, however, Murphy's Law took effect. Everything that could go wrong, went wrong—in the worst way. I had made the decision, though battling in my flesh, to let go of the sheets.

Devastating News

Now in the meantime, I had to go back to Michigan to get my immunization shots so that I could fly overseas. While I was there, one of my friends called to say, "Guess what happened to your friend today?" I said, "What? Did he die?" My friend's response devastated me. "No. He got married."

How could he get married when he and I were dating? I couldn't even cry. I dropped to my knees and crawled from the kitchen to my bedroom. I couldn't say a word. My emotions throbbed with the pain of betrayal. He was the second boyfriend who had done this to me.

What should I do? Should I stay in Michigan and hide, or leave? I felt trapped there. I had to go back to that city and face it. I had to deal with everybody knowing that I was his woman, but actually I was not his woman; I was his sheets. That's all I was. I was a high-class prostitute who got paid very well. I was a call girl.

∽

IF YOU KNOW THE LORD AND YOU
STILL DO NOT GLORIFY HIM, YOU WILL
OFTEN FIND YOURSELF IN A MESS.

∽

You Must Dismantle

I know that I am talking to somebody reading this book. Listen to me. If a man really loves you, he will not touch you. If he loves you, he will respect you. I know what I am talking about because I have gone through it.

Things did not work out for me after that. I had to pray and ask God how to get out of the situation. This is the point that I am trying to make by writing this book. Just because a relationship doesn't work out or there is a break-up, doesn't mean that the sheet is gone. I had to ask God, "What do I have to do to get out of the sheet?" This is when the Lord told me that first of all, I had to get rid of all of the devil's deeds.

I had to go and throw all of the clothes out. I remember when I walked into my mother's kitchen and pulled out everything he ever bought me and threw it in the middle of the floor. I yelled and told everyone to come and get what they wanted. I didn't want any of it. I even gave the car away. These were the beginning stages of my purification.

I knew that I could not keep anything in my house that was going to feed the demon of loneliness and remind me of what he used to be to me. For God to heal me and for me to step into the purpose He had for my life, I had to take the other person off of the throne of my heart. I had to put God back on the throne. That meant I had to dismantle everything.

∞

WHEN YOU THINK ABOUT AN EX ALL THE TIME, THE DEVIL IS SETTING YOU UP. DON'T GIVE ANY PLACE TO THE DEVIL TO DRAW YOU BACK INTO SIN.

∞

God Will Make a Way

The Lord graciously provided a way of escape from the pain of dealing with this man's marriage. There's a price to be paid when you walk in unrighteousness, and I paid dearly. God, in His mercy, did not allow me to suffer long. Within a month's time, Pan American called me to Miami for six weeks of training to become a flight attendant.

That's where I found a church called Jesus People. I walked into a service and heard a pastor named Isaiah Williams' teach about selling out to God. "Make sure that you don't give the devil any place." He continued, "God has great things in store for some people in this building. As long as you view what the enemy has as being more valuable than what God has, you will never embrace what God has for you."

∞

AS LONG AS YOU VIEW WHAT THE
ENEMY HAS AS BEING MORE VALUABLE
THAN WHAT GOD HAS, YOU WILL
NEVER EMBRACE WHAT GOD HAS
FOR YOU.

∞

It was so weird that I walked into that church in 1988 and heard a teaching that spoke directly to me. I returned to that church many times while training in Miami and was greatly blessed. Years later, I was invited to speak at Sister Williams' women's conference, one of the largest conferences in this country. I never knew in 1988 that our paths would cross again. God is so merciful to those who are His.

After training in Miami, I was transferred to New York City. I didn't know anyone in that city, and I didn't know where I would stay. But I watched the hand of God—from day one—make a way where there was no way. God prepared a place for me in the presence of my enemies. God carved a passageway for me in the desert and provided water in dry places. I have watched the hand of the Lord over and over and over again.

You may ask, "How can the hand of the Lord be for you when you were so against the hand of the Lord?" I believe one particular incident started those miracles in my life. I had to do a very courageous thing—I had to humble myself. Because I had not legally been released from my past shepherd, I had to ask for his forgiveness. I had already been hired in New York and had officially moved. However, I called my pastor so that the curse and the spirit of rebellion would be lifted from my life.

∞

HUMBLE YOURSELF BEFORE THE LORD.

∞

Did you hear that? You must be—*must be*—properly passed on to your next level by your former shepherd, legally. I had to go back and apologize. Let's see what the Word says about rebellion and stubbornness.

> *For rebellion is as the sin of witchcraft, and stubbornness is as iniquity and idolatry. Because though hast rejected the word of the Lord, He hath also rejected thee from being king* (1 Samuel 15:23).

If you are operating in witchcraft, everything you touch just crumbles. No doors can be properly opened for you. Even if the doors open, you will have a hard time walking through. You will have difficulties in everything you do. The Lord made me aware of that. So, I called my former pastor and repented to him before God.

He said, "Juanita, I will keep you in my prayers." He promised, "I'll ask God to lead you to a new shepherd in New York. Until then, why don't you call me on a weekly basis?"

∞

WHEN YOU OPERATE IN WITCHCRAFT, EVERYTHING YOU TOUCH CRUMBLES, NO DOORS CAN BE PROPERLY OPENED FOR YOU, AND YOU ARE HEADED FOR A FALL.

∞

When you start all over again—learning how to trust God from scratch—you go from having everything to having nothing. That's very traumatic. Sometimes the best way for God to refocus you and retrain your mind is to have you gutted out. God has to make sure that no other spirit is in competition with His Spirit. When you hit rock bottom, sometimes all you have is your hope in God. You can still trust the One who made you.

When you have a repentant heart that is turned toward Jesus, remember that He cares for His own. In New York, I discovered God as Jehovah Jireh, my Provider. And oh boy, did I!

∞

GOD CARES FOR ALL WHO REPENT AND TURN THEIR HEARTS TO HIM.

∞

My employer gave us two weeks to find a place to live in New York, which is a very difficult thing to do. Until then, we stayed in a hotel. Other flight attendants had already been to New York or had friends there. Some were prepared for this, but I didn't have a clue. I called a girlfriend who lived in Philadelphia to ask if I could stay with her until I found a place in New York. I knew that I could take the short train ride between the two cities. My friend agreed. When I hung up the telephone, I lay across the hotel bed and began to talk to God.

"God, I don't have any more money for hotel rooms. Tomorrow I need to be out of this hotel, and I don't know where I'm going." Within hours, a young man called me. A mutual friend gave him my number. He had a room to rent. I told my roommate from training, who also hadn't yet found a place to stay, that we could get twin beds and move in together. Crying, she thanked me.

We gathered our things and moved there. It was not in the best of neighborhoods. Neither of us was comfortable in that environment. She was from a very well-to-do family. I was from Chicago. My family wasn't wealthy, but we weren't "dirt poor," either.

I knew I was in boot camp then. God had placed me there for a reason so I didn't complain. It was a little bedroom and the living conditions weren't ideal. But in my spirit I had peace. I knew that the Lord had made a way for me to have this place out of the purity of my spirit. You don't know how good it felt for me not to owe anyone for anything. It was because of the Lord. It wasn't the Ritz, but it was what I had birthed out during the beginning stages of my purification.

Better is the poor that walketh in his integrity, than he that is perverse in his lips, and is a fool (Proverbs 19:1).

The Residue Remained

After a few months of living in New York, I got on a plane one day and a man asked me if I would like to be a call girl, making $700 a call. Now get this, because this is powerful: What made him ask me that? Simply put, the residue of that old spirit was still on me. He was a Caucasian guy who did not know me from Adam. He told me that he had been watching me during the flight. His supervisor had asked him to find someone, and I looked like a person who might be interested. He told me that they worked out of downtown Manhattan. He went on to tell me that the girls and guys that worked for the organization entertained very wealthy people. He asked again would I like to become a professional call girl. He told me that they would buy all of my outfits, and I would live in a penthouse with them.

Now, I ask again: What would make him ask a saved, sanctified, Holy Spirit-filled girl like me a question like that? He saw the residue on me. I had just come from being highly paid. It was another chief who knew the spirit that was on me. That was the Lord's way of saying that I was not completely cleansed yet.

I was going through the right process, but there was more to it than that. There is responsibility on both parts. There is responsibility on the part of God, and there is responsibility on the part of you as an individual. I had done a fraction of my part. I had gotten rid of all of the clothes and material things. I had gotten rid of all the boyfriends and phone numbers. I was even willing to walk in poverty, but I needed to be in a ministry that preached and operated in deliverance so that the spirit could be cast off me. It was still hovering around me, and I needed to be a part of a ministry that could break that filthy residue off of me. The anointing had to be heavy enough to go to the depths of my spirit and get the root, because if we don't get the root, it will grow back again.

It was not until I walked into New Greater Bethel Ministries, when Pastor Boyd began to preach and teach deliverance, that things began to change. Not only was God taking me through self-deliverance, but there was still more. Let me tell you how I came to find my spiritual home.

Finding a Church

During this season, I visited different churches, but I didn't find what I was looking for. I went without a church home for the first six months. During this time, I realized that I could live holy—I mean really saved. I was extremely surprised. I was shocked that I had a desire to read my Bible and to get on my knees every day and pray.

I turned on the radio one day and heard the ministry of New Greater Bethel Ministries. Their broadcast aired three times a day on WWRL. They played the song "Just Be Patient and Wait on the Lord" every day. Tears spilled out of my eyes each time I heard it sung. The voice of the prophetic flowed heavily in that ministry. Every time I listened, the preaching seemed to be designed just for me. For six months, I listened to this church on the radio.

When I flew out of town, I went to my hotel room and searched for a local Christian radio station. Lo and behold, there it was—New Greater Bethel. This church had a nationwide broadcast. This was so timely for my journey. God reached out and cared for me even in a strange city. He was determined not to let me be without a current word in my belly.

Now, here comes my miracle. Listen to this: One Sunday morning, I reported to work and the supervisor said that I wasn't due to fly out until 7:00 p.m. so I left the airport and had breakfast. It was October 11, and I vividly remember that it was a brisk day. As I started back home, I was one block from my house when I noticed a woman standing at the bus stop with her three children. They looked so cold as they huddled there.

The Holy Spirit spoke to me and said, "Turn around and give them a ride. They are on their way to church."

I noticed that my gas tank was on empty. I thought, "I have enough gas to make it to work and then home." My pockets held no more than 30 cents. When I hesitated, the Lord reminded me, "I've brought you this far. Give that lady a ride."

I turned around, pulled alongside the curb, and said, "Ma'am, you're saved, aren't you?"

"Yes, I am," she said.

"The Holy Spirit just told me that you're out here waiting for a bus. I'm supposed to give you a ride to church."

"Thank you," she said. "I just missed our church bus and the church is quite a distance from here. But for some reason, I felt that I had to get to church today."

On the way, she noticed my gas gauge. "Pull over there," she said as she pointed to a service station. "I want to buy you some gas. I just don't want to miss church today." I got out, smiled through the windshield and tore it up speaking in tongues and thanking the Lord for that gas! You see, some people may think you're crazy, but you must learn to thank Him for gas and anything else He does for you while you're walking through a desperate situation.

When I filled my tank, this woman handed me $20. "The Lord told me to do that for you," she replied. And you know I tore it up again in the praise!

I couldn't help but say, "God, look at how You are working!"

When we got to church, she invited me in, but I hesitated. Still wearing my airline uniform, I knew I wasn't dressed for church. "Just come as you are, honey," she said smiling.

Walking into that church, I got the greatest surprise of my life. Standing there was the preacher I had been listening to on the radio for six months! Guess what the soloist was singing when I walked in? That's right: "Just Be Patient and Wait on the Lord."

People didn't know what was wrong with me. Before I even got to my seat, I was sobbing. When the pastor got up to preach, he said, "There's someone in this church who is like an eagle whose wings have been broken, but God says He's going to heal your wings. Your worst days are behind you, and your best days are yet to come."

By the time he finished prophesying and looking in my direction, I was underneath the pew and under the power of God. When I came to, I began to weep and praise God because *I knew I was home.* I had found a shepherd. I was no longer open prey for the enemy. God had led me to someone who would watch over my soul. I knew that I was standing in the perfect will of God. After I joined myself to that ministry, many wonderful things began to happen. I can't even begin to name them all.

Eventually, I went to my pastor in New York and began to share with him my entire story. I didn't keep any secrets. I had to tell the truth as to how I had messed up because I did not want him harboring a fugitive in the church. I didn't want to be a Jonah on the ship, wreaking havoc at my church.

It's Your Turn

Wait one moment. You aren't reading this book by chance. It's not because you watched the "No More Sheets" video. You're reading this book because it's your season; it's your turn. God is not going to leave you exposed to the enemy. He doesn't want you to be wandering in the wilderness, open prey for the crafty one. Your life doesn't have to be devoured.

❧

You are reading this book because it's your season—it's your turn. God will not let the enemy devour your life.

❧

Just like you're reading my story, there's a story behind your life. There's a plan that God has for you. Right now, the Lord is earmarking people and destinations where you are going to be birthed into the fullness of your calling. Your miracle is going to come to pass. You will know home when you get there. You will know your shepherd when you see him. You will know the voice of God when you hear it. I prophesy to you right now, "The Lord is in control of your life. Fear not. What the enemy meant for your harm, the Lord is turning around for your good."

❧

I prophesy to you: "The Lord is in control of your life. Fear not. What the enemy meant for your harm, the Lord is turning around for your good."

❧

Looking back over my life, I know this Scripture is true.

And we know that all things work together for good to them that love God, to them who are the called according to His purpose (Romans 8:28).

Remember the training in Miami? Pastor Williams ministered to me, and later God used me to deposit some things into the lives of his flock. All things work together for good. Every detail of your life fits into God's eternal plan.

✖

EVERY DETAIL OF YOUR LIFE WILL
WORK TOGETHER FOR YOUR GOOD.

✖

If God has a destiny for your life, shouldn't you begin to prepare for it? Once you crawl out of the sheets, you'll find a lot more work to do. Yes, it's a big job. Yes, it requires faith and sacrifice. But if you make room for the Master, your life will never be the same.

CHAPTER SIX

The Process to Purification

Behold, I will send My messenger, and he shall prepare the way before Me: and the Lord, whom ye seek, shall suddenly come to His temple, even the messenger of the covenant, whom ye delight in: behold, He shall come, saith the Lord of hosts (Malachi 3:1).

The Lord really ministered that Scripture to me. It wasn't until I finally began to really seek after God that He suddenly came into His temple, which is my body. The Scripture tells us that our bodies are the temple of the Holy Spirit (see 1 Cor. 3:16-17).

But who may abide the day of His coming? and who shall stand when He appeareth? for He is like a refiner's fire, and like fullers' soap: and He shall sit as a refiner and purifier of silver: and He shall purify the sons of Levi, and purge them as gold and silver, that they may offer unto the Lord an offering in righteousness (Malachi 3:2-3).

The difference between the words *purify* and *purge* is powerful. Purify means "to make clean," but the word purge means to cleanse harshly.[1] God was letting me know back then that when He enters in, I must get rid of every connection to sin. When the Lord comes back in, He is going to purify me and make me clean, but this time it is going to be a harsh purging. (Please bear with me because I am going to feel the pain of this coming out.)

❧

PURIFY MEANS "TO MAKE CLEAN."
PURGE MEANS TO CLEANSE HARSHLY.

❧

He was letting me know that there are really going to be some lonely days and very lonely nights. There will be some travailing. There must be a time of prayer and much Scripture reading. There must be much time spent in church. While in church during worship service, you will feel the residue lifting off of you. In other words, this will be a process.

It will not feel good. But just as a woman goes through pain while having a baby and the result of the pain makes her so very happy, so will it be with you. You will be able to say, "I am in pain, but I am in pain because I am being delivered. I am emptying out all of the junk that the enemy has put inside of me. I am emptying out all the sheets that were left in me. I am being washed with the fuller's soap—a very strong soap used in Biblical days. The Spirit of God is purifying me. I am being purged by the Holy Spirit."

∞

Cleanse me, O Lord, and give me a new start.

∞

Discerning the Body

Watch this! Remember that after you have gone through this, you will offer up unto the Lord an offering in righteousness. Well, the Scripture then begins to talk about your finances and discernment.

> *Then they that feared the Lord spake often one to another: and the Lord hearkened, and heard it, and a book of remembrance was written before Him for them that feared the Lord, and that thought upon His name* (Malachi 3:16).

The Lord not only heard them, but He put it in a book of remembrance. That meant that when He looked in that book, He was reminded of their request. Now, you must notice they talked about *the Lord continually* and not about George or Willie and how he rocked your world. They did not talk about how many times He made them *scream out His name.*

> *And they shall be Mine, saith the Lord of hosts, in that day when I make up My jewels; and I will spare them, as a man spareth his own son that serveth him* (Malachi 3:17).

The Scripture says that they thought upon the name of the Lord. They were not daydreaming about Sam; they were concentrating on the goodness of Jesus. People who constantly have their minds on the Word are the Lord's people.

Then shall ye return, and discern between the righteous and the wicked, between him that serveth God and him that serveth Him not (Malachi 3:18).

Look at how powerful that verse is. The Lord is going to give you back your power to discern. When you begin to speak one to another and fear the Lord, your conversation then belongs to God. You are honoring God. You're praising God. He puts it in the book of remembrance, and for a reward, He calls you His.

Not only does He call you His, He also turns around and brings restoration to your power to discern. When He does that, you're able to discern what is good and what is evil, what is God and what is not. You're no longer deceived by calling things that are of the devil, God. You're no longer deceived by the spirit of divination or by the devil's craftiness and his work.

When you look at people, you're able to tell right off—before you get mixed up with the wrong crowd—if that person is bearing the fruit of the Holy Spirit. You can discern that. You're not tricked again by the next Joe Blow or by the next Susie that comes along talking about, "I think you're my husband. I think you're my wife. Can we date? Can we go together?" You will see by way of discernment that they are not right—that it's a setup from the devil. You will recognize that this is the wickedness of the enemy.

❧

YOUR DISCERNMENT WILL BE "OFF"
UNTIL YOU ARE PURGED
AND PURIFIED.

❧

And how do I know? I have been purified. Not only have I been purified, I've allowed God to take me to the next level of purification, which is purging. I've been cleansed to the point that my spirit and my mind are no longer tainted. I'm no longer operating out of the residue of the flesh from my past. I'm operating out of the power and the discernment of the Holy Spirit.

An example of a harsh cleansing is this: Sometimes when we come out of sin, we want to embrace the thing that we came out of. Understand something: you're a person who is stronger than you think. Listen, if you had strength to stay in the world and survive among demons, you can't allow the enemy to trick you and make you think that now that you're saved, you're so timid.

Isn't it strange that the first time the pastor wants to correct you, give you a Scripture, or rebuke you, you're ready to declare how sensitive you are. You want to leave the church. You want him to say it a little softer than that. But while you were in the world, you took people cussing you out and still kept going back to the same bar.

See, you have to understand something: When the leadership—whoever is going to mentor you and assist you in your walk with the Lord—corrects you, they see a spirit. They are not coming after you; they are after the residue that they see. You must understand the love of God. He chastens whom He loves (see Heb. 12:6).

The Training Phase

Look at this example: Malachi 3:1 talks about the messenger who will come. Who is the messenger? The messenger is the trainer. The trainer is the refiner. When you have made the decision to be saved, and you begin to submit yourself to much fasting and prayer, you are in boot camp.

Like the Bible said, the refiner, which is the trainer, will come, and he will begin to *teach your spirit*. That is why you can't get saved from an in-depth life of sin and make decisions on your own. The Word says everything has to be done through prayer and supplication (see Phil. 4:6).

At this point, the Lord will begin to tell you things. The Spirit of the Lord in your belly will convict you and will tell you, "Take it off. That's too short. That's too low. That's too sexy. That's too appealing. That's not of Me." It takes you going through this process to be able to hear the voice of God. Your flesh has a loud voice; it's got a big mouth. It doesn't want to die anyway.

The average person who gets saved wants to continue to do as many things as they used to and still profess salvation! When you've lived a life of sin, you must come *all* the way out. You are not a person who can live a borderline life. You are not a person who can take a chance. When you know you have a problem with your flesh, you can't test the waters.

∽

YOU CANNOT AFFORD TO LIVE A BORDERLINE LIFE.

∽

You can't go with Johnny or Jimmy every now and then because that's your chief. A person who smokes can't visit a tobacco factory. A person who has an alcohol problem can't go to a wine-tasting event. Forget about it; *that's your chief.* You have to stay away from the atmosphere your chief lives in.

If your chief is sex, then you have to come away from porn movies to get that spirit off you. You can't sit and watch television—where people are putting their tongues down one another's throats—and think you're going to survive. What is really happening is that you are starting to feed the flesh again and you are giving it an appetite for more. (Like I said in the previous chapter, here we go again!)

You must pay close attention to what I am about to say. According to Ephesians 2:2, satan is the power and the prince of this world—which means he has the legal right to rule in it. Now where he does not have a right to rule is any place where the Holy Spirit resides. That place is off limits. If he crosses the line, we then have a legal right to rebuke him, because now he is on God's property.

❧

WHEN SATAN'S DEVICES ARE AT WORK, REFUSE TO BE USED BY THEM. EVEN WHEN YOU FEEL WEAK, GOD IS THERE.

❧

It is so important that we be *in* this world, but not allow our lifestyles to be of this world.

> *Don't copy the behavior and customs of this world, but be a new and different person with a fresh newness in all you do and think. Then you will learn from your own experience how His ways will really satisfy you* (Romans 12:2 TLB).

This is why Paul wrote: *"Therefore if any man be in Christ, he is a new creature: old things are passed away; behold, all things are become new"* (2 Cor. 5:17).

Every time the U.S. government signs or passes a law condoning things that are not according to the Word of God, we have legalized satan's tactics. We cannot tell him where he can and cannot operate. This is why when Congress passes laws for gay rights, the spirit of perversion runs rampant. Apparently, lawmakers have forgotten that the Spirit is also entitled to the White House. The only way we, as a people, will not be affected by perversion, inordinate affections, and illicit sex acts is this: we must be filled with the Holy Spirit so that no other spirit can enter in.

The Harsh Purge

Everything that sits before you—the company that you keep, what you watch, what you read, and where you go—has got to be steered toward your end result, which is your deliverance.

I have been harshly purged a number of times. There were times I felt like giving up. There were times I'd been rebuked by my pastor for going out with unsaved men. I would leave and go home and say, "I ain't coming back to church, because he embarrassed me." Actually, the demons were embarrassed. The spirits became exposed from my bathing in fuller's soap and they didn't like it.

Remember when I left Michigan, went home to Chicago, and stayed there? It was only a couple of weeks before the Lord began to let me know that I wasn't this embarrassed when I was sleeping around. You were not embarrassed when you let somebody see your naked body. You were not embarrassed of your filthy mouth.

Understand this: Rebuke is good for you because it causes you to understand God. It causes you to know that God *ain't playing*. It causes you to know that He loves you. When there's a mandate on your life for the nations, God doesn't have time to spoon-feed you. You almost don't have time for milk and cereal. He has to do a quick work in you.

A quick work will always be a harsh work. Due to the lateness of the hour, and the shortness of time, we must redeem time. Everybody who's going to take this death walk of the flesh is going to be cleansed harshly. Therefore, you better get ready for it!

God is going to require that you make quantum leaps in Him. Today you may be sucking a bottle and tomorrow you may be on steak. What causes this change is your ability to say "Yes" to everything that He puts before you. When you say, "Yes, Lord," and begin to praise God and discuss the greatness of God, it helps your spirit to digest the will of God.

The quicker you can digest His Word, the better. Once God realizes that you can retain it and your spiritual body can hold on to what He says, then God will say, "OK, now you're ready for some cereal." After you've retained that, He says, "Now you're ready for steak."

Your level of maturity in God is not measured in years. It is revealed in your "Yes, Lord." After you have done all of the above things, *"Then shall the offering of Judah* [Judah means "praise"] *and Jerusalem be pleasant unto the Lord, as in the days of old, and as in former years"* (Mal. 3:4).

> *And I will come near to you to judgment; and I will be a swift witness against the sorcerers* [meaning that when the devil throws spirits of witchcraft and mess at you to hinder where you are going in God, God is going to be a witness against them and say, "Not so"], *and against the adulterers* [every fornicating devil that's coming after your flesh to entangle you again in bondage], *and against false swearers* [everyone who puts their mouth against you], *and against those that oppress the hireling in his wages* [the boss that's doing you wrong],

the widow [if you've lost your husband and the enemy is coming against you, He's going to say, "Not so"], *and the fatherless* [if you are a child who doesn't have a father or doesn't know where he is, God's going to rebuke the enemy and stand as a witness against that spirit. He's going to say, "Not so"], *and that turn aside the stranger from his right, and fear not Me, saith the Lord of hosts. For I am the Lord, I change not; therefore ye sons of Jacob are not consumed* (Malachi 3:5-6).

All of the above is going to happen when you say, "Yes, Lord, purge me and purify me. Take a seat in my spirit and refine me with fuller's soap."

∞

YOUR LEVEL OF MATURITY IN GOD
IS NOT MEASURED IN YEARS. IT IS
REVEALED IN YOUR "YES, LORD."

∞

Now I want you to lift your hands right there and tell Him, "Yes." Before we go any further tell Him, "Yes." Come on. The minute you say, "Yes," you're going to take another step. The minute you say, "Yes," you're going from kindergarten to the sixth grade!

Purified and Processed

I told you we are going to do quantum leaps, not baby steps. There's enough power in a "Yes, Lord" to launch you as far out in God as you want to go. One thing about it, you cannot be launched beyond your Word level. The Word of God in your spirit, mixed with a "Yes, Lord," launches you into places of eternity. You can experience things in the realm of the Spirit of God that you have never experienced before—not by your emotions or by tapping into realms of familiar spirits. The Word of God allows you to travel closer to the revelation of God. There, He begins to reveal Himself to those that have been purified and processed.

At this point, He can trust that you're not a covenant-breaker. He can trust you not to tell His secrets. In reaching the level you wish to reach, your chariot ride into new places will be swift. He does not come to purify your emotions. He comes to purify your spirit so that your new spirit can control your life.

∞

GOD DOESN'T COME TO PURIFY
YOUR EMOTIONS. HE COMES TO
PURIFY YOUR SPIRIT SO THAT YOUR
NEW SPIRIT CAN CONTROL YOUR
EMOTIONS—AND YOUR LIFE.

∞

For many of you who are constantly crying, the Lord just spoke to my spirit and said, "Without the process of purification, without purging, without allowing the Word to take a seat in you, and without the washing of the fuller's soap, you have no right to demand a defender." You have no right to demand God to correct any situation because your father is satan. Being purged protects you, defends you, purifies you, and empowers you. That's how that goes; it's an exchange. Our Heavenly Father takes care of His own.

When the devil comes against you, you must have power to rebuke him. You're a body fighting against itself. Once you have been purified and cleansed of the spirit of the enemy, then the spirit of the enemy becomes your enemy. That means there's enmity between you and that spirit. Enmity means hate.

∽

Rebuke that spirit and decree that you will awake to righteousness and not sin.

∽

You must understand this: It takes strength to die in the Lord. While you are young and have the strength to go through the process of purification and purging, you should. It takes strength to be able to fast. Why do you think we have older people with serious character problems?

∽

To overcome, you've got to fast. You don't have a choice.

∽

While you have strength in your body to pray three or four hours, or go on a 10- or 21-day fast, you must commit yourself to do it. Hurry up and allow God to take you through the process of purification before you get too old to be processed. Now that you've begun the process in your inner person, let's look at the rest of the benefits behind this operation.

You Can Change Your Destiny

And I will rebuke the devourer for your sakes, and he shall not destroy the fruits of your ground; neither shall your vine cast her fruit before the time in the field, saith the Lord of hosts.

And all nations shall call you blessed: for ye shall be a delight-some land, saith the Lord of hosts (Malachi 3:11-12).

You can change your destiny. You don't have to sleep with anyone for a lamp. You don't have to let anyone feel on you for clothes. There is a process which God intends for you to follow.

❧

WHEN YOU BUY THINGS FOR
YOURSELF, YOU CAN HOLD YOUR
HEAD HIGH BECAUSE YOU DIDN'T
HAVE TO SLEEP WITH ANYONE TO GET
THEM. ALL YOU PAID WAS CASH.

❧

Now, if you do it His way, you're going to be blessed; but if you do it any other way, you will surely be cursed. After you've gone through His process, then other aspects of your life will fall into place. There are things in your character that will begin to reflect the manifestation of the process.

Let me give you an example of what I'm trying to say. There are people who have received titles in the Church and find themselves pressed for people to respect their title. When what is manifesting in your character is not appropriate with your title, people will call you what they see.

As I began to yield to the purification and the purging of the Holy Spirit, people automatically began to call me Evangelist Bynum or Prophetess Bynum. I didn't have to say, "Excuse me. Don't disrespect me by calling me Juanita." You don't demand honor. Honor is given when the manifestation of that honor is operating in you. The Bible says that after you go through the process, nations will call you blessed. Your name will change and they will recognize your calling.

Now remember, the word *purge* means to cleanse harshly. I must remind you that in order to be "pure" gold, fire must be applied. Let me explain to you how this works. The goldsmith grabs a piece of gold, sticks it in the fire, and turns up the heat. The fire then melts the gold and all the impurities in the gold come to the surface because of the high temperature. Those impurities and black spots are then scraped off the top of the gold. This process is repeated over and over again until it is pure gold. That gold has been made clean through a purging.

This means if God's going to purify you then you are going to have to lose the chips on your shoulder. You are going to have to be able to take rebuke and correction. You are going to have to refuse the watered-down version of the Word. You must match the strength of the Word with the depths of sin that you were in.

You cannot live in sin for ten years and want to walk in God with a mere piece of a Sunday morning message and think you're going to survive. You have to be processed back into your divine state. You gave the devil time to process you out of your divine state. Now, you must give God the same amount of years to process you back to Him.

You have no legal right to say that the Word doesn't work until you have given it the same amount of time that you gave sin! Remember, when you are slightly constipated, you take a mild laxative; but when there's continued constipation—and all kinds of impurities have built up in the colon—you require a colonic irrigation. You've *got* to get all that cleaned out! That is a harsh cleansing. Whatever you present to God after this point, it is done in righteousness—whether it be money or whether it be serving in the Church.

Endnote

1. Dictionary.com. s.v. "Purify"; s.v. "purge." http://dictionary.reference.com/browse/purify and http://dictionary.reference.com/browse/purge (accessed: January 04, 2010).

CHAPTER SEVEN

Inordinate Affections

My people are destroyed for lack of knowledge: because thou hast rejected knowledge, I will also reject thee, that thou shalt be no priest to Me: seeing thou hast forgotten the law of thy God, I will also forget thy children (Hosea 4:6).

Look at this: the Scripture did not say they didn't have knowledge. It says the people of God are destroyed for *lack* of knowledge.

Lack means not enough. You have some knowledge, but you don't have enough to keep you from destruction. He said, "What I did was create a whole universe, and I put things over the entire world so that you may know Me."

Whether you go to Spain, South Africa, Japan, or Brazil, there is no part of the world you can visit that does not have a part of the creation of God. He has to make sure that the knowledge of who He is clearly seen by what He has made. I don't care where you go. You will find an example of who God is.

You ask, "How did I get myself in this mess?" Romans 1:21 says: "*…When they knew God, they glorified Him not as God, neither were thankful; but became vain in their imaginations, and their foolish heart was darkened.*"

∞

REMEMBERING YOUR STRUGGLES
AND VICTORIES HELPS TO KEEP YOU
CONSCIOUS OF WHO YOU ARE AND
WHAT YOU ARE DOING.

∞

The people became vain. Self was lifting up self. They became like satan. I will, I will, I will, I will. Follow me closely with the Scripture. If you have enough time to go with me through these Scriptures, please do so.

> *How art thou fallen from heaven, O Lucifer, son of the morning! how art thou cut down to the ground, which didst weaken the nations! For thou hast said in thine heart, I will ascend into heaven, I will exalt my throne above the stars of God: I will sit also upon the mount of the congregation, in the sides of the north: I will ascend above the heights of the clouds; I will be like the most High. Yet thou shalt be brought down to hell, to the sides of the pit. They that see thee shall narrowly look upon thee, and consider thee, saying, Is this the man that made the earth to tremble, that did shake kingdoms; that made the world as a wilderness, and destroyed the cities thereof; that opened not the house of his prisoners? (Isaiah 14:12-17)*

The Lord asked lucifer (satan), "How did you lose your spot, son of the morning?" Lucifer was a glorified being. He had stones and jewels in his body. He was gorgeous, and he even dwelled among the heavens with God.

Now watch this: We know that there is no sin or iniquity in Heaven. How did satan get removed from the heavens because of sin, if there was no sin and no opportunity to sin? Because every creature of the Lord is made with its own will.

When the angels were made, they were made with exquisite expertise and glory. Their eyes and their spirits were actually created. They were face-to-face with a glorified God. They *chose,* out of *their* will to sing, "Hosanna to the King" and to bow down before Him. It was so much glory in God until they magnified Him all day and all night. They had never seen anything like that before. However, lucifer was such a gorgeous being until he got beside himself and he wanted to be praised.

Now let's look at the image of lucifer. There were wind pipes in his body. I can imagine when the winds blew in the heavens, his body made music. He was a worshiper and he was made more beautiful than any of the angels that were ever made.

The Bible says, *"How art thou fallen from heaven, O Lucifer, son of the morning!"...* [This is how it happened:] *"For thou hast said in thine heart, I **will** ascend into heaven, I **will** exalt my throne above the stars of God: I **will** sit also upon the mount of the congregation, in the sides of the north: I **will** ascend above the heights of the clouds; I **will** be like the most High"* (Isa. 14:12-14, emphasis added).

He said, "I will." *The minute he began to turn to his will instead of the Lord's will, he had to come down.*

How'd I Get Into This Mess Again?

How was it that I was in the sheets one more time? Like lucifer, I turned from *Thy* will to *my* will. I had an opportunity to know God, and I did not seek the knowledge that I might not be destroyed. I needed to know how *to know God* so I began to ask.

But I became vain in my imaginations and my foolish heart was darkened. Watch this: I professed myself to be wise and became a fool.

And changed the glory of the uncorruptible God into an image made like to corruptible man, and to birds, and fourfooted beasts, and creeping things (Romans 1:23).

The Scripture is saying that he diminished who God was and began to look at creation as nothing. The average mind says, "I planted some corn, therefore I got a corn field," never thinking that God allowed all the elements to come together in that soil to create that corn. The minute you begin to ignore the magnitude of who God is and begin to bring the power of God and the greatness of God to a human level, you equate yourself with God.

Therefore, you have every right to believe in your heart that there is no hope for you, because there isn't. The minute God becomes as you are, you don't have any hope. You must always keep God in the position of being more than you, so you can have somebody to reach up to.

∞

THE MINUTE YOU RECOGNIZE HIM AS BEING THE GREATER POWER, THEN THE EXAMINATION OF YOUR HEART CAN BEGIN.

∞

Dishonoring Our Own Bodies

Here is what happened to me: When I got up in the morning—the minute I opened my eyes—did I say, "Lord, I thank You for waking me"? No. I began to walk in vain glory and actually began to steal the glory from God. That was and is a very serious matter. To be honest, that was how I got with Mr. Man. That was how I got promiscuous. This is how *we* become sex symbols.

Paul said, *"Wherefore God also gave them up to uncleanness through the lusts of their own hearts, to dishonour their own bodies between themselves…"* (Rom. 1:24).

∞

YOU ARE IN A BATTLE TO REGAIN
THE RESPECT OF YOUR BODY.

∞

You dishonored Him as God, and it backfired on you. If you will not respect God, then you will not have respect for your body. Likewise, you are not going to have respect for anyone else, nor anyone else's body. The Word teaches, "I'm going to cause you to dishonor your body, because you didn't honor My body."

Who changed the truth of God into a lie, and worshipped and served the creature more than the Creator, who is blessed for ever. Amen. For this cause God gave them up unto vile affections: for even their women did change the natural use into that which is against nature: and likewise also the men, leaving the natural use of the woman, burned in their lust one toward another; men with men working that which is unseemly, and receiving in themselves that recompence of their error which was meet (Romans 1:25-27).

Those whom God gave up became lesbians and homosexuals. The women and men went against nature. Women had no more need for the law of the creation.

The Bible always requires that the male leave his father and his mother and cleave to his wife (see Gen. 2:24). However, due to their own foolishness, the men left the natural use of a woman. This was the total opposite of the instruction from God. The Lord's instructions were to leave mother and father. He didn't say leave women.

The beginning of man's destruction is when he started walking in rebellion to what the will of the Father was. But here, because of his own imagination and his lack of respect to the body of God, men began to leave the women and burn in lust one toward another.

> *And even as they did not like to retain God in their knowl-*
> *edge, God gave them over to a reprobate mind, to do those*
> *things which are not convenient...* (Romans 1:28).

Now, let's look at the word *retain*. When you go to an attorney, he normally asks for a retainer. The retainer means that he wants some guaranteed money. His thinking is, "This money is going to hold my interests on your case. It's going to keep me from wandering off and doing other things. As long as I have your retainer, I'm going to work on your behalf even though you haven't paid me enough to hold me in position." When we retain God, we may not have all of Him, but we have enough of Him to hold us in position.

Remember, people are destroyed for lack of knowledge. The people whom the apostle Paul was talking about didn't want to get a clear understanding of God—or they did not want to hold on to that understanding. Therefore, God gave them over to a reprobate mind to do those things which were not convenient. What is a reprobate mind? It is to exchange the truth for a lie and believe it to be the truth. You've experienced a lie as being the truth for so long until you start believing it.

❧

When you have a reprobate mind, you exchange the truth for a lie.

❧

We are going to know God by gaining the knowledge of the way He created us. The wife receives a deposit from the husband which produces a child. This is the reason the Bible calls the plan of salvation being born again.

You may say, "My grandma was a nymphomaniac. My daddy was a whoremonger along with all of my uncles. It's just in my blood." But upon receiving a blood transfusion from the blood of Jesus Christ, old things have passed away; behold, all things—my blood system, my heritage, the way I look, the way I talk, the way I act—are become new (see 2 Cor. 5:17).

❧

Apply the blood of the Lamb to the doorposts of your heart. The death that comes from sin and transgression will pass over your life.

❧

This is why the Word insists that we (me and you) must be born again! I hope I'm helping you right now. Let's continue a little further with the Scripture.

Being filled with all unrighteousness, fornication, wickedness, covetousness, maliciousness; full of envy, murder, debate, deceit, malignity; whisperers, backbiters, haters of God, despiteful, proud, boasters, inventors of evil things

[This is where all the little toys come in—the electronic toys that people use in all this backward, promiscuous, sexual activity. I know somebody just said in their mind, "Don't go there." Oh yeah! I'm going there. Evil things are sex gadgets or anything that you can use that's contrary to the natural law of God.], *disobedient to parents* [Whenever you find a teenager that's outright rebellious and disobedient, they have involved themselves in an unnatural affection, whether it's of the above mentioned things or not.] (Romans 1:29-30).

Natural means the nature of God. Unnatural means against the nature of God. In Christ, God Himself has a nature for us.

Second Peter 1:8-12 says:

For if these things be in you, and abound, they make you that ye shall neither be barren nor unfruitful in the knowledge of our Lord Jesus Christ. But he that lacketh these things is blind, and cannot see afar off, and hath forgotten that he was purged from his old sins. Wherefore the rather, brethren, give diligence to make your calling and election sure: for if ye do these things, ye shall never fall: for so an entrance shall be ministered unto you abundantly into the everlasting kingdom of our Lord and Saviour Jesus Christ. Wherefore I will not be negligent to put you always in remembrance of these things, though ye know them, and be established in the present truth.

Abound means to stay there. If the Word stays there, you won't be barren or unfruitful in the knowledge of our Lord Jesus Christ. This is what makes you go back to sin and back to the sheets. When all of the things that God has for you in His nature don't stay in you; you become empty. You begin to forget that you were delivered. You begin to forget that God broke that spirit out of you when you were slain under the power. You are a person who people will *call* a Christian, but they see no manifestation in your lifestyle or your deeds.

∞

WHEN YOUR LIFESTYLE AND DEEDS
DON'T REFLECT YOUR SALVATION,
THE ONLY ONE WHO KNOWS YOU ARE
SAVED IS YOU.

∞

There is no fruit because you lack knowledge, temperance, patience, virtue, or faith. You don't have enough of these things. No one knows that you are a Christian but you. That's why you have to constantly tell people that you are a Christian. When you have enough of these things, the glory of the Lord will be upon you, and your light will shine and people will see your good works and glorify your Father who is in Heaven.

Without understanding, covenantbreakers, without natural affection, implacable, unmerciful: who knowing the judgment of God, that they which commit such things are worthy of death, not only do the same, but have pleasure in them that do them (Romans 1:31-32).

∞

PEOPLE WITHOUT UNDERSTANDING
ARE COVENANT BREAKERS.

∞

Beware the Consequences

Now let's look at another Scripture:

...Awake thou that sleepest, and arise from the dead, and Christ shall give thee light. See then that ye walk circumspectly, not as fools, but as wise, redeeming the time, because the days are evil. Wherefore be ye not unwise, but understanding what the will of the Lord is (Ephesians 5:14-17).

The Word warns you to beware the consequences of what you are doing. Now, that's powerful! If you were walking circumspectly, you would know you're going to die if you continue to go in the same direction. You should know that such things are worthy of death. This verse says they are walking as fools who think that they have forever to live. Not so! In the very next verse, it tells us to redeem the time for the days are short.

∞

Beware the consequences of sin.

∞

Romans 1:32 says that these people are having pleasure in the mess. Do you know what that means? How can you have joy in the company of those who walk with no conscience if you know the judgment that comes behind them? When you are processed out, you don't have joy in the company of anyone who becomes involved in anything that is worthy of death.

For example, why do we refuse so strongly to associate with people we know sell drugs? There are other things listed in Scripture that are more deadly. We have gotten to a point where we want to indulge ourselves with the pleasures of our own flesh. There is a very important concept that you must conquer when dealing with the power of the problem.

Knowing Enough of God

You must earn the privilege of walking out the deliverance that you speak of. Many of us have not paid the price, but we want the results. Every time you get out of the bed and say, "I'm not going to do it anymore," you have to back that up with a question: "Have I paid the price to stay out of the bed?" You haven't earned the ground to say, "I'm not going to do it anymore." You lack too much knowledge of who God is. That is exactly why you do it again and again.

Contrary to what the Scripture states in Second Peter the first chapter, you are barren. You may know of God and of peace. You may know of joy and even know of deliverance. But you don't know enough of deliverance to say, "I won't do it anymore." Knowing enough of God is knowing enough to walk circumspectly and realize that if I do this, then I'm going to die.

> *But ye have not so learned Christ; if so be that ye have heard Him, and have been taught by Him, as the truth is in Jesus: that ye put off concerning the former conversation the old man, which is corrupt according to the deceitful lusts; and be renewed in the spirit of your mind; and that ye put on the new man, which after God is created in righteousness and true holiness. Wherefore putting away lying, speak every man truth with his neighbour: for we are members one of another* (Ephesians 4:20-25).

I am talking about hearing His voice. I can hear some people now saying, "I need a word of prophecy; I need a prophet." No—you need a Bible! Hear Him through His Word. The real truth is the Word. You have to put away the former conversation of the old man, which is corrupt according to the deceitful lust. From this knowledge, you will change how you talk and who you talk to.

❦

You might say, "I need a prophecy; I need a prophet." No—you need a Bible! Hear Him through His Word.

❦

You have to cease from vain babbling and vain conversation. Why? Because your conversation will speak out of the residue of the lust of your flesh, which is not purified. You will begin to sit up and talk sex and junk. Put away the conversation of the old man and be renewed in the spirit of your mind. How does that happen? It happens through the Word.

This is the way you put on the new man: you put on the new man by searching for him through the Word. How is this man made? He is made after God, who *is* Righteousness and True Holiness. When you find truth in God's Word, it is a seed that is planted in your heart.

❦

Put away your former conversation—stop talking about sex and foolishness.

❦

You must be careful to protect your seed. You must work on your own life to protect your position in God. You must work on your life as a single person and get to know yourself all over again. *You must spend quality time with yourself.* I know for many of you, that is a spooky thing, but you must learn your weaknesses and your strengths so that you are no longer deceived. As my uncle use to say, "You have to know the rabbit and the rabbit's habits!"

You can no longer afford to feed yourself junk. Everything that comes on television or radio may not be something you can allow into your spirit. We have all been designed and structured differently. Our levels of tolerance are different. You must learn that what your home girls may do, may not be something you can embrace and still live to tell the story. You must know yourself to the degree that you are able to look a situation in the face and determine that it's not for you.

∽

YOU MUST PROTECT YOUR
PURIFICATION AND YOUR POSITION
IN GOD.

∽

CHAPTER EIGHT

Elements of Salvation

There are three elements to the plan of salvation: justification, regeneration, and sanctification. You cannot be saved without having experienced each.

Justification means that you have been acquitted and the offenses of the sin in your life are erased as if you never did it. That means when you stand before God, there are no telltale signs that you used to be a lesbian or a homosexual. There is no proof that you used to smoke cigarettes or were a drug addict. When you walk in the full operation of justification, there should be no appearance of any part of your old lifestyle. In other words, it should be a secret unless you want to tell it.

> *And for this cause He is the mediator of the new testament, that by means of death, for the redemption of the transgressions that were under the first testament, they which are called might receive the promise of eternal inheritance. For where a testament is, there must also of necessity be the death of the testator. For a testament is of force after men*

are dead: otherwise it is of no strength at all while the tes-
tator liveth (Hebrews 9:15-17).

There is a revelation in having a testimony. What makes a testimony have power is when there is a death of the testator. It gives him a testimony. He talks about what he died to and what he was resurrected into. If you die in it, it is buried and is no longer a part of you. Therefore, when you testify, you resurrect the memory of what God has done for you. That's why you have a testimony. When you have been saved two or three years, we should not be able to look at you and tell that you were a drug addict or a prostitute.

When the people of old went out and told of the works of Jesus, people were convinced. Do you know why? They saw a man with blind eyes see and a lame man walk. They were convinced about the authenticity of Jesus when they saw the manifestation of miracles in the lives of those who witnessed about Him.

Someone who has had problems in their walk with God can say, "I used to smoke two packs a day. I used to be a prostitute, but now I am justified." That's a gift that comes along with salvation. Justification makes you look as if you have never been a sinner. It makes you look as if you have never been a liar, a cheater, or a prisoner. You have been justified by the faith of Christ. Therefore, you have *peace* with God.

∞

JUSTIFICATION MEANS THAT YOU
HAVE BEEN ACQUITTED.

∞

Regeneration ties in with justification. I have been regenerated in my soul where sin operated, ruled, and abided. My soul realm is where I learned iniquity and I learned the iniquity through the soulish relationships of my family. That iniquity was transformed or transmitted into my spirit which made me dead to God. When I got regenerated, I was given a new spirit and my soul was renewed.

Regeneration causes me to be adopted into a new family. That's the point where your momma isn't your momma, your daddy isn't your daddy, and your family isn't your family. You have been adopted into the royal family.

All of your uncles may have been alcoholics, but *you* have been justified and regenerated. Everybody in your family may be on welfare, but when you get justified and regenerated, you get a blood transfusion and a new inheritance. Now, you don't have to be what your family is, but you will be what your Father in Heaven is. That's powerful.

Maybe someone in your family has died from cancer. Someone in *that* family, but now you're adopted into the royal family. Cancer does not run in *this* family. TB doesn't run in your new family. HIV doesn't run in your new family.

Sanctification goes along with justification and regeneration. It means you no longer have to walk according to your natural family lineage, but you will be what your Father in Heaven is. Now that's *powerful!* This means you have been made to sit in right relationship to God's laws. You have been born again to a new life—bought with a price—therefore you are not your own person.

❦

SANCTIFICATION MEANS THAT YOU
HAVE BEEN SET ASIDE TO SERVE
THE LORD.

❦

Sanctification means that you have been set aside to serve the Lord because He paid for you and you are owned by Him. *When He regenerated you, you were adopted into His house.* He went to the adoption agency, adopted you, and took you to His house. Once you get in His house—because you are so thankful that you're not in an orphanage anymore—you promise to serve Him. Serving Him doesn't mean nursing, ushering, or collecting the offering. Serving Him means that you have now become dedicated to the altar.

> *I beseech you therefore, brethren, by the mercies of God, that ye present your bodies a living sacrifice, holy, acceptable unto God, which is your reasonable service* (Romans 12:1).

∽

DELIVERANCE IS SOMETIMES IMMEDIATE, BUT SANCTIFICATION IS AN ONGOING PROCESS.

∽

My dedication and my sanctification mean that I have been glued for eternity to the altar. I have dedicated myself to the point where I vow that I will serve Him until I die. A *saved* person is *one who has been set right with God, adopted in the divine family, and is now dedicated to God's service.*

∽

HAVE YOU WANDERED AWAY FROM YOUR VOWS TO THE LORD?

∽

Now, it's getting ready to get heavier than that: Being *justified* says you belong to the righteous. Being *regenerated* says you are a child of God. Being *sanctified* says you are made holy. You are not born holy. You are made holy. You were forgiven and justified as if you never sinned.

I hear people say this a lot: "No one tells me whether I am saved or not. No one tells me how to dress." Well, maybe they don't, but your actions speak for you. The outward change called justification is followed by an inward change called regeneration; this, in turn, is followed by your dedication to God's service.

We must be careful when we start saying things like this: "I have been justified. I have been regenerated. I have been sanctified." We must realize now that we are walking through the operation of sanctification, which means, when we came to the altar, and received the Word, we were justified and regenerated.

∽

YOU ARE NOT BORN HOLY. YOU ARE MADE HOLY.

∽

Next, I was baptized in the Holy Ghost. It's not about chills up your back and goose bumps down your legs; it is about the Spirit. The Lord is saying, "Now I've done the work, but in order for Me to keep you, I've got to submerge your spirit in My Spirit. You have to be so far under until none of you is seen."

Have you ever gone swimming? I'm not talking about in three feet of water with a cute swimming suit on. When you dive in, if you don't stay with the flow and the technique of being under water, you are going to die. You're not in eight feet of water playing when you've just learned how to swim.

How do you stay in the deep without killing yourself? The only way is to keep treading water. Your feet and hand actions must change.

Here, the water represents the Holy Spirit. Everything about you looks different when you're submerged in water. You are not a busybody under water, nor do you mess with other folks under water. You're trying to figure out how to stay alive. You are not trying to play footsie with anyone in eight feet of water, are you? I didn't think so!

Baptism With Fire

The Bible says that you don't have to seek for the Holy Spirit for He is a gift.

> *Then Peter said unto them, Repent, and be baptized every one of you in the name of Jesus Christ for the remission of sins, and ye shall receive the gift of the Holy Ghost* (Acts 2:38).

The Holy Spirit first fell on believers on the day of Pentecost. The saints were in one accord in one place—the upper room. Jesus had sent them to a designated place—a place that was away from their family, phone, television, and junk.

> *And, behold, I send the promise of My Father upon you: but tarry ye in the city of Jerusalem, until ye be endued with power from on high* (Luke 24:49).

He sent them among people whose desires were the same. They were all hungry for the Holy Spirit.

> *And when the day of Pentecost was fully come, they were all with one accord in one place. And suddenly there came a sound from heaven as of a rushing mighty wind, and it filled all the house where they were sitting. And there appeared unto them cloven tongues like as of fire, and it sat upon each of them. And they were all filled with the Holy*

Ghost, and began to speak with other tongues, as the Spirit gave them utterance (Acts 2:1-4).

The Bible says that the Holy Spirit fell when they were all in one accord. Now what am I saying? We are body, soul, and spirit. Your body has to be submitted to the fact that your soul is hungry and thirsty for the Holy Spirit, and your spirit desires Him.

∞

YOUR BODY MUST SUBMIT TO THE
FACT THAT YOU NOW HUNGER AND
THIRST FOR RIGHTEOUSNESS.

∞

When body, soul, and spirit all get together in one place with one aim, the Holy Spirit will fall on you. The gift of the Holy Spirit will manifest Himself in you.

But the Comforter, which is the Holy Ghost, whom the Father will send in my name, He shall teach you all things, and bring all things to your remembrance, whatsoever I have said unto you (John 14:26).

The Bible says that the Holy Ghost is a teacher. How do I know? I have Him. There is a voice in the depths of your soul and it's talking to you. It is leading and guiding you. There's an unction that comes up and tells you don't do this, or don't do that, put that down, don't touch that, don't go here, turn that off, don't watch that, and don't taste that. This is a true manifestation. The Holy Spirit does not only come in, but here is where He *resides.*

CHAPTER NINE

Masturbation

This is one of those subjects that people don't like to talk about. It has been one of the most controversial subjects in Christendom. There has been debate back and forth: Should Christians masturbate? Should Christians not masturbate? Is it safe for Christians to masturbate? Is it wrong for Christians to masturbate? Well, I chose to write about the subject of masturbation because I've done it!

Now first, before we go on, pick your face up off the floor and glue it back on your head and let us continue! See, this is exactly what I'm talking about. This is why most of our single people are going to the dogs and sexual promiscuity is taking over our churches. Everybody wants to sit in the pulpit and sit under choir robes and pretend that they've never done anything.

Right now, believe me when I tell you, writing this is not an easy thing to do. This is very painful. I almost didn't write it. Two weeks prior, I encountered a young person who was being so tormented by that spirit until it broke my heart. My mind went back to the passage in the Bible when the blind man said,

"I once was blind, but now I see." Those words caused others to believe in the power of Jesus.

More than you can imagine, I want whoever's reading this book to be *set free!* Being that this subject is so controversial, I chose to write this chapter based on my own experience. When I get through explaining to you what the Holy Spirit has revealed to me, concerning me, not you—because remember you don't do anything—then I'll let you decide, based on my experience, whether you should or should not masturbate!

Before we go to our first Scripture, let me give you a visualization of how I look in the stores. See if this sounds familiar to you: I walk in the Christian book store the morning after I've masturbated. I want deliverance, so I'm looking for a book on masturbation.

I finally locate it against the wall, *Masturbation and You,* but when I go to pick it up, another Christian sister or brother walks in the same section reading something in a topical Bible. I don't want them to see me pick that book up! When they finally walk away, I pick it up and start browsing through it, while looking over my shoulder to see if anyone notices me reading it. I come to the conclusion that there are some powerful things in it that could really help me!

I walk to the counter and the clerk says, "Next."

I then ask myself, "Am I crazy? When I lay this book on the counter, they're going to know I have a problem with masturbation." So then I say, "Never mind," as I lay the book down *anywhere* in the store and walk out! Now, does that sound like you?

I've decided to enter this chapter in my book—but I hid it. So you can pick up *No More Sheets,* race to this chapter, get delivered, and nobody will ever know!

Second Peter 1:1-2 says:

Simon Peter, a servant and an apostle of Jesus Christ, to them that have obtained like precious faith with us through the righteousness of God and our Saviour Jesus Christ: grace and peace be multiplied unto you through the knowledge of God, and of Jesus our Lord....

❦

IF JESUS WERE RIGHT THERE, YOU WOULDN'T DO OR SAY CERTAIN THINGS. WELL, HE IS THERE! HE SAID "I WILL NEVER LEAVE THEE..." (HEBREWS 13:5).

❦

The Definition

Through my own experience, I have understood that a clear definition of masturbation is the bait that satan uses to become a master of you! This spirit forces you to relive past sexual relationships or future fantasies. And what happens is this: When the physical sensation is over, the pain of the reality is now in your face. That's when you realize that the hurt has not healed.

❦

MASTURBATION: THE BAIT THE DEVIL USES TO MASTER YOU AND SEND YOU TO HELL WITH THE SPIRIT OF YOUR MIND—A FORM OF DEATH BY YOUR OWN HANDS.

❦

Hear this: Many times people feel that when they masturbate, it's just a physical exercise. That is a far cry from being the truth because when you indulge in this act, you actually have to go into the spirit of your mind. This is why the Bible says to be renewed by the spirit of your mind.

In the seat of the spirit of your mind—where the imagination of the Lord does not reside and where impure thoughts are—there is the evil working of the enemy in the thought realm. When you travel into that realm to such a depth that you cause a physical sensation, you have tampered with demons in a realm that you know not of.

❨❩

WHEN YOU MASTURBATE, YOU ARE
ALLOWING A SPIRIT TO AROUSE YOU.
YOUR SPIRIT IS WIDE OPEN AND
YOU DON'T KNOW WHAT SPIRIT OF
PERVERSION HAS JUMPED INSIDE YOU.

❨❩

But, my brothers and sisters, there is a problem and a very big one. From my own experience with this, I noticed a few months after indulging in this kind of activity, my spirit got really ugly. My personality began to change. I became brassy and cocky and just ridiculously outspoken.

So you may be asking yourself, "When will that happen?" When you have a desire for companionship, you begin to work on yourself both spiritually and naturally. You do not refrain from things that will turn a good man away. I'm not talking about a heathen; I'm talking about a good man.

"I Don't Need a Man!"

Listen to this: All of a sudden, I started not really being tight about looking the best that I could or conducting myself like a class act. You see, the whole spirit of that can cause you to cut purpose out of your life. Not only will you start feeling like you're all right, but you'll respond incorrectly.

For example, a really nice friend could say something like, "You know, you are really getting fluffy." (I got that from Bishop Carlton Pearson—by the way it's another word for *fat*. Ha! Ha!) Your comment would be, "So, I ain't looking for nobody." Here come the famous words: "I don't want nobody. Anyways, I ain't never got to be married!" *Bam!* There it is! Inside, you really do want to be noticed. You really do want to be married.

Girlfriend, do not play yourself like that! You know deep down within, you want companionship, but you feel it's much easier to masturbate and remain undefined than to work on your character.

You get with your girlfriends and then everything becomes, "Girl, we can do this!" If it's putting a roof on the house we say, "Oh I can do it." Cleaning the garage? "Oh, I can do that, too." I don't care how you look at it; you cannot cut the desire for a man out of the lives of real women! Any woman who says, "I can, I can, I can, and I don't need a man," is headed for a big trick.

❧

YOU HAVE A DECISION TO MAKE.
ARE YOU GOING TO MEET YOUR OWN
NEEDS, OR ASK GOD TO SEND A
MATE TO MEET THOSE NEEDS? IT'S UP
TO YOU.

❧

I remember one day, me and my God sisters were cleaning out the garage. We were throwing out boxes and moving things around. We had gotten nowhere near halfway finished before my back started hurting, my arms started hurting, and blisters were developing on my fingers.

After breaking three nails and feeling fatigued, I turned around to all of them and said, "Are we crazy? We need a man!" The way it came out of my mouth was so comical that everyone fell out laughing and said, "Girl, why you right?" We realized we can't live without brothers.

I can almost guarantee that the continuation of that kind of activity will soon result in your body's form and shape to begin to take the form of a man! This is why you must be careful because what the enemy will try to do—within the realm of deception—is get you to move, lift, and shove things that were designed for the strength of a man.

Once you begin to tear those muscles, about six months to a year down the road, you will realize that your body structure is beginning to change. Your features will become more masculine; the way you walk, the way you talk, the way you sit, and the way you hold your hands will become identical to that of a man.

Have you ever considered why a man looks like a man? Because he's trained from childhood to take out the garbage and to lift heavy things that will constantly put an overload on his muscles. So by the time he's 18, 19, or 20 years old, his body has actually structured itself to look like a masculine man.

When women begin to perform the same duties that are meant for the strength of a man, their bodies will begin to change as well. This is the biggest deception that I've ever seen of satan. This is the reason why when I need things to be done around the house that *far supersede my limitations as a feminine woman—as a real woman—I call on a real man.*

Sisters, in Chapter Eleven, I discuss why we must stop molesting and seducing our brothers—I'm talking about our brothers in Christ. If every brother ends up being your potential husband, then who can you call on to just be a brother? Yes, we ask our brothers in the Lord to come over and help us. But, get this: The rule is, bring your wife, kids, and everybody because if you don't, "trick-ation" will take over.

I don't know about the rest of you all reading this book, but I thank God for men. You may be asking yourself, "Is that the reason she's got braces at 39 and is losing weight?" Yep! Yep! Yep! 'Cause I do want a man!

After my deliverance, I worked for years on my inner woman and my character. I picked back up the burden of reconstructing myself, and it was not easy and still isn't easy. But through the power of the Word, I have made quantum leaps within my person. I had to make the adjustment in my mind that if God didn't ever allow me to marry, He wanted me whole and healed! That meant I had to let God heal me and deliver my thought life!

> *Casting down imaginations, and every high thing that exalteth itself against the knowledge of God, and bringing into captivity every thought to the obedience of Christ...* (2 Corinthians 10:5).

Let me just say this: The trips and the journeys that you go through in your mind to reach an orgasm is what the Bible means when it says casting down imaginations and every high thing that exalts itself against, against, against the proper method of doing things. And the proper method of doing things is doing them in the knowledge of God.

∞

YOUR IMAGINATION CAN BE USED AS
A SETUP TO ENTRAP YOU.

∞

Now listen: I just took a moment and said to myself, "Every time you do this, you have to repent. Now if I'm going to God to repent for unclean thoughts, then I'm by myself because sin is sin and wrong is wrong."

Spiritual Perversion

You may ask, "Which is the lesser of two evils?" Well now, brace yourself for what I'm about to say. First of all, only marriage is honorable and the bed is undefiled. But when you are with a man, you have become tied to his soul.

When you reach an orgasm from the realm of imagination, you have traveled into the spirit realm for that climax. You are out of control, your body is responding to that act, and you don't know what spirits from that realm have entered you.

I believe that the first spirit that enters in is perversion. Why do I say that? Because you get up feeling, "I'm all right. I don't need nobody else but me!" That, my brothers and sisters, becomes spiritual perversion. What is perversion? Turning away from the natural use of a thing that God created and embracing the wrong method as right.

∞

DON'T EVEN FOOL YOURSELF.
MASTURBATION AND PORNOGRAPHY
WILL NEVER BE ENOUGH TO
SATISFY YOU.

∞

Now, I know right there you got to just lay this book down for a minute and take a deep breath. I know how you must be feeling right now. Remember, I feel it every day and the challenge of being cleansed and staying cleansed becomes a decision; do I want to get my thoughts and my mind messed up and my flesh screaming out all over again after it has been asleep? No! *So I get up, put a worship CD on "continuous," and go to sleep, because it's really not worth it. Remember, it takes a few minutes to do it, but days and weeks to erase it.* **That's just too much drama for me!**

Here I go, back into the presence of God. That was the hardest thing for me knowing that I had to face God looking like Jethro from The Beverly Hillbillies facing Granny when he knew he had just done something stupid. Did you hear what I said? I had to face God, not man. I just got tired of going to God saying in the terms of ebonics, "God, this is me. I know what You had said, but...! Oh God, I feel like a dog."

It just makes your spirit feel so torn up, until, brothers and sisters, it ain't worth the residue that it leaves. Your thoughts are being weighted with guilt and shame. You're battling in your mind with the mental negativity you were exposed to. You're digging up all the pain from the *memories* of what it used to be like.

You then begin to realize that you could have really been using those sections of your brain to reconstruct your future. That's why I say that I believe that the true definition for masturbation is the fact that you become a slave to your past and ugly, ungodly imaginations. I am not saying that you are not going to be tempted and tried by this spirit, because you are! I am and everybody who is not married is.

I beseech you therefore, brethren, by the mercies of God, that
ye present your bodies a living sacrifice, holy, acceptable unto

187

God, which is your reasonable service. And be not conformed
to this world: but be ye transformed by the renewing of your
mind, that ye may prove what is that good, and acceptable,
and perfect, will of God (Romans 12:1-2).

Put on the New Man

Daily, daily, daily, daily, daily you must constantly remind
yourself of what His Word says about your thoughts!

And be renewed in the spirit of your mind; and that ye put
on the new man, which after God is created in righteous-
ness and true holiness (Ephesians 4:23-24).

Do you see that—put on a new man (or woman)? If I am
commanded by the Word to put on a new woman, the Spirit
of the Lord is certainly not commanding me to put on a new
woman with an old mind!

The Word of God states, in Matthew 9:17, that we should
not put new wine in old wine skins. The two don't mix! If I am
to put on a new woman, I must be renewed in the spirit of my
mind or else my old mind will take my new woman back to its
old nature, which is death.

For they that are after the flesh do mind the things of the
flesh; but they that are after the Spirit the things of the
Spirit. For to be carnally minded is death; but to be spiri-
tually minded is life and peace. Because the carnal mind is
enmity against God: for it is not subject to the law of God,
neither indeed can be. So then they that are in the flesh
cannot please God. But ye are not in the flesh, but in the
Spirit, if so be that the Spirit of God dwell in you. Now
if any man have not the Spirit of Christ, he is none of His
(Romans 8:5-9).

People Are Spirit

Remember in Chapter Eight when we talked about being saved? Let me give you a little diagram that the Lord showed me in a dream.

People do not have a spirit. People *are* spirit, and within them is a soul that lives in a body. Now, this is what happens:

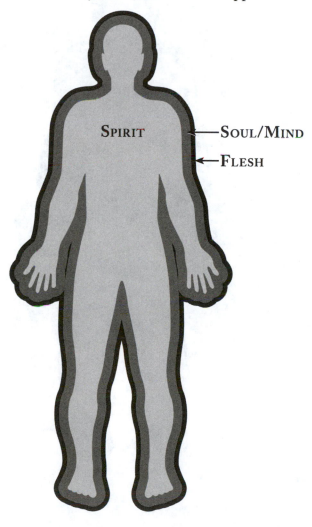

When God saves (rescues) your spirit, He comes with His Spirit and totally takes over your dead spirit. Your spirit is dead because of sin. It becomes alive because now God is there.

Now, in order for the Spirit of God to become as large as the soul and the flesh—which were ruling before you got saved—you must begin to renew your mind. Where does this take place? In your mind.

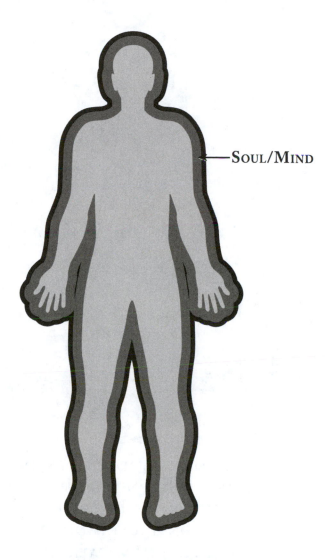

SOUL/MIND

With God sitting within your spirit and the Word of God renewing and transforming your mind—you guessed it—the flesh begins to line up with the Spirit of God. The flesh has to be trained to live a new lifestyle according to the Word of God.

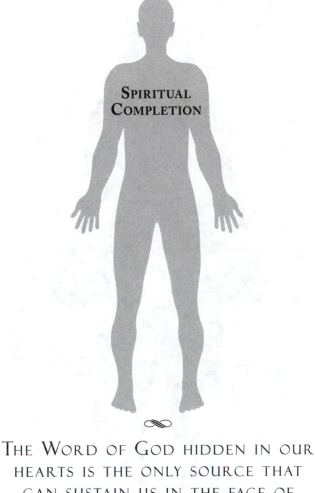

THE WORD OF GOD HIDDEN IN OUR
HEARTS IS THE ONLY SOURCE THAT
CAN SUSTAIN US IN THE FACE OF
CONTINUED AND
FUTURE TEMPTATION.

If you ever try to go about this process backward, you will keep failing over and over again. Why? Because your flesh and your own self-willed mind—which was formed and shaped in iniquity—have been in partnership all of your life.

Now, what is iniquity? Remember, I said it is doing anything without God being in it.

So, the spirit was dead, dark, and lifeless. The soul and flesh just took over and did and said whatever they wanted to do and say.

Now, here's the shocker: God steps into your spirit and saves it. The spirit starts to dictate to the mind, which is your conscience, "I don't want to walk and operate in lust and damnation anymore." Your will says "Yes" to the Spirit of God. At this point, the mind and the will begin to search the Word of God. When God's Word goes in, the mind is transformed and it breaks the news to the flesh: "We are saved and we will be a holy vessel." You will see that with time, you too can become new.

Yes, the flesh is going to cut up and get mad. You see, it has lost its holding place, which was a dead spirit. To walk in sin is death. So, if as a sinner you were dead in trespasses and sin—and sin is ruling in your mind and flesh—then what or who can stop you from sinning? No one.

But, the minute Christ steps in, light and life shine out from within you and expose the deeds of satan. Daniel 2:22 says, *"He revealeth the deep and secret things: He knoweth what is in the darkness, and the light dwelleth with Him."* Then, when the Word in your mind connects to the Spirit of God in your spirit, the curse of sin is broken. Bam! You've been set free.

This is what makes you a Christian—not just jumping and shouting for the moment because the music is loud. All of that is good in its rightful place, my brothers and sisters. But, after the singing and shouting, if you don't get the Word of God inside, the Spirit of God will not stay. He will come into an unclean temple to clean it, but He will not stay inside one that does not practice and exercise itself in cleanliness.

∽

WHEN YOU RETURN TO THINGS THAT
ARE UNGODLY, YOU ARE RETURNING
TO WHAT IS STILL IN YOUR SOUL.

∽

This is where you experience what the Bible calls backsliding. It's like pushing the reverse button and taking your life back to the era when you did not know God. Let's properly describe masturbation: It's like eating vomit. Proverbs 26:11 says, *"As a dog returneth to his vomit, so a fool returneth to his folly."* Second Peter 2:22 reiterates that: *"But it is happened unto them according to the true proverb, The dog is turned to his own vomit again; and the sow that was washed to her wallowing in the mire."*

You may be asking this question: Why is it that some spirits can just come out, but it takes others *so* long? Well, the answer is simple. When the Spirit of God first started calling you away or warning you not to walk into that trap, you ignored the voice of God and the Word of God. So now that you have been forgiven, you walk in a penalty for the rebellion.

Don't let anybody tell you differently. God forgives you, but there is a penalty you pay for rebellion—even if it's mental warfare. The mind must be completely renewed and the flesh retrained. But I'm your witness—the closer you get to God and the more you stay in His Word, the quicker you come out. If you are serious about what you are reading, I suggest you get your tennis shoes on and walk your hips right out while your penalty is minor. Think about it. You already have to pay some kind of penalty—don't add to it.

> *This I say then, Walk in the Spirit, and ye shall not fulfill the lust of the flesh. For the flesh lusteth against the Spirit, and the Spirit against the flesh: and these are contrary the one to the other: so that ye cannot do the things that ye would. But if ye be led of the Spirit, ye are not under the law. Now the works of the flesh are manifest, which are these; Adultery, fornication, uncleanness, lasciviousness, idolatry, witchcraft, hatred, variance, emulations, wrath, strife, seditions, heresies, envyings, murders, drunkenness, revellings, and such like: of the which I tell you before, as I have also told you in time past, that they which do such things shall not inherit the kingdom of God. But the fruit of the Spirit is love, joy, peace, longsuffering, gentleness, goodness, faith, meekness, temperance: against such there is no law. And they that are Christ's have crucified the flesh with the affections and lusts. If we live in the Spirit, let us also walk in the Spirit* (Galatians 5:16-25).

So if the flesh is referred to as being attached to the carnal mind, which is death, and the carnal mind is what is used to masturbate the flesh, then I had to ask myself a question. According to this passage of Scripture, how can masturbation be of God? And I say again—you don't have to debate with me—I was instructed by the Spirit of the Lord to expose me so that you may have an opportunity to view the other side. Is it painful for me? *Very!*

Someone may say, "Don't you think people are going to look at you funny? In the carnality of their minds, they may visualize you performing such an ungodly act." Sure, some will. But like Jesus on the cross, at some point before His death, He had to be seen as ungodly that He might save the world.

One powerful thing that I found out is this: Masturbation will cause the devil to master you. The enemy will allow you to get involved with someone who is not God's will for your life just to be able to use your mind. He wants to store the memory of an ungodly act in your mind—only to sever the relationship—so that he can use the memory to push your flesh into an ungodly act without the person even being present. With ungodly thoughts, the enemy can send you destruction by using your own mind to dictate to your hand. That's what you call death by your own hand.

> *Blessed is the man that endureth temptation: for when he is tried, he shall receive the crown of life, which the Lord hath promised to them that love Him. Let no man say when he is tempted, I am tempted of God: for God cannot be tempted with evil, neither tempteth He any man: but every man is tempted, when he is drawn away of his own lust, and enticed. Then when lust hath conceived, it bringeth forth sin: and sin, when it is finished, bringeth forth death* (James 1:12-15).

Do you see that? If you can stop the conception, then masturbation and lust will *never be born!* What does it mean to be drawn away of your own lust? When you are living right, and you are walking in the Word, you are waiting on the Lord.

But then you might sit down one night and turn on HBO at 2:00 A.M. and up pops a movie where a couple is throwing down, gettin' it! Now, there is no "Robocop" standing over you with a gun drawn to your head. Remember, you have the remote control in your hand, and when you make the decision not to turn the channel to Nick at Nite, then you have been drawn away by your own decision; that means you have been enticed by the enemy to open up that door again.

❧

LUST IS AN INSATIABLE SPIRIT AND
AN UNAPPEASABLE WORK OF
THE FLESH.

❧

Once lust has conceived—meaning that you have wished in your heart that you could get involved in sexual immorality again—then you've allowed the seed to be planted, and it has already begun to grow. Lust that's been conceived brings forth sin. If you receive what the Word of God is saying, you will live, but if you reject what God's Word is saying, you will be drawn away. The Word states to us that the wages that sin pays is death, but the gift that God gives, which is the plan of salvation, is eternal life! (See Romans 6:23.)

❧

IF YOU'RE FLIPPING THROUGH THE
CHANNELS AND WATCHING SEX
ACTS, YOU ARE BEING ENTICED AND
DRAWN AWAY BY YOUR OWN LUST.

❧

The Spirit of the Past

If, in fact, acts of lust and lustful imaginations exist because of the spirit of your mind, don't allow your mind to be open to the spirit of the past. While you are out there reminiscing, you have left the reality of the now and transcended into the spiritual. If that spiritual realm is not in the realm of God, then you have just exposed your spirit to a satanic realm that has more to offer than just a sensation. Meaning? Once the act is finished, the only thing that has been satisfied is the physical. You either struggled through the thoughts of the past, or you tapped into another realm.

∽

DON'T ALLOW YOUR MIND TO BE
OPEN TO THE SPIRIT OF YOUR PAST.

∽

If you went into the fantasy land of the future, the enemy expanded the corruption of your mind into an area that you have not even experienced yet. Now there is a strong, subconscious sexual drive. The enemy will not stop until that fantasy becomes a reality. This is why we must be renewed in the spirit of our mind.

Casting down imaginations, and every high thing that exalteth itself against the knowledge of God, and bringing into captivity every thought to the obedience of Christ... (2 Corinthians 10:5).

Remember ye not the former things, neither consider the things of old (Isaiah 43:18).

What Should You Think On?

Philippians 2:5 says, *"Let this mind be in you, which was also in Christ Jesus...."* So you may ask yourself, "Then what should I think on?" Philippians 4:8-9 has the answer:

Finally, brethren, whatsoever things are true, whatsoever things are honest, whatsoever things are just, whatsoever things are pure, whatsoever things are lovely, whatsoever things are of good report; if there be any virtue, and if there be any praise, think on these things. Those things, which ye have both learned, and received, and heard, and seen in me, do: and the God of peace shall be with you.

Did you understand that? Those things that you've learned, seen, and heard of the Lord...think on those things.

For as he thinketh in his heart, so is he: Eat and drink, saith he to thee; but his heart is not with thee (Proverbs 23:7).

Wherever you put your concentration and your focus, that is what you become. So the deception of the enemy is to keep you thinking about things in your mind that are impure—things that have no good report, things that are not just, and things that are not filled with virtue—so that you don't become those godly things. He wants you to think of all the ungodly things because the more ungodliness you think about, the more ungodly you become. The more you think on things pertaining to the things of God, the more like God you become.

∽◦∽

GET UP OFF YOUR BACKSIDE AND
SPEAK THE WORD OF GOD
OVER YOURSELF.

∽◦∽

This is why we must make sure that our thoughts line up with who Christ says we are. We must take that thought and say, "satan, I rebuke you in Jesus' name. I cast this thing out of my mind. I am operating with a pure mind and pure thoughts and according to the Word of God. I am going to let the mind of Christ be in me."

❀

ANYTHING CONTRARY TO THE
WILL OF GOD MUST BE CAST
DOWN, WHETHER IT BE IDEOLOGIES,
DOCTRINES, TRADITIONS, OR WAYS
IN WHICH WE WERE RAISED.

❀

Remember, the enemy is not going to stop tempting you. Never, never, never! He wants back in, and the only way to get in is to tempt and entice. First he says, "I must get the appetite so strong that the desire becomes overwhelming, until they can't resist." So you must not think badly about yourself because you are tempted. You are supposed to be tempted.

❀

TEMPTATION IS NOT WRONG.
YIELDING TO TEMPTATION IS WRONG.

❀

I remember a phrase from a song my grandmother used to sing: "Yield not to temptation for yielding is sin..." The temptation is not the sin. It's the *yielding* to the temptation that is sin!

My brethren, count it all joy when ye fall into divers temptations; knowing this, that the trying of your faith worketh patience. But let patience have her perfect work, that ye may be perfect and entire, wanting nothing. If any of you lack wisdom, let him ask of God, that giveth to all men liberally, and upbraideth not; and it shall be given him... Blessed is the man that endureth temptation: for when he is tried, he shall receive the crown of life, which the Lord hath promised to them that love Him (James 1:2-5,12).

200

Why rejoice at temptation? Because God has already given you power to escape it. What do you allow to occupy your mind? OK, let's look at this Scripture again:

Finally, brethren, whatsoever things are true, whatsoever things are honest, whatsoever things are just, whatsoever things are pure, whatsoever things are lovely, whatsoever things are of good report; if there be any virtue, and if there be any praise, think on these things (Philippians 4:8).

That word *virtue* shows up in Scripture a lot. *Virtue* is the exercise of righteousness and moral goodness. Thoughts of someone in go-go boots, with whips and chains, tied to a bed and screaming, are not thoughts of things that are pure and full of virtue.

∽

WHAT YOU CHOOSE TO THINK ABOUT
IS A DECISION *YOU* MUST MAKE

∽

OK, now let's look at another Scripture:

These six things doth the Lord hate: yea, seven are an abomination unto Him: a proud look, a lying tongue, and hands that shed innocent blood, an heart that deviseth wicked imaginations, feet that be swift in running to mischief, a false witness that speaketh lies, and he that soweth discord among brethren (Proverbs 6:16-19).

Did you see that: an heart that deviseth wicked imaginations? In other words, *deviseth* means created, and *mischief* means trouble.

∞

THOUGHTS OF SOMEONE IN GO-GO
BOOTS, WITH WHIPS AND CHAINS,
TIED TO A BED AND SCREAMING, ARE
NOT THOUGHTS THAT YOU SHOULD
DWELL ON.

∞

Keeping Your Conversation Chaste

Remember that we talked about stooping to our lower nature? There are several things that cause us to revert and one is our conversation. This is why we must keep our conversation chaste. I am a firm believer that there are some things that occur when you don't keep your conversation clean. This is backed up by the Word of God:

A wholesome tongue is a tree of life: but perverseness therein is a breach in the spirit (Proverbs 15:4).

Perverse conversation causes a breaking in the spirit. Let's say that God is moving and flowing in your life, causing things to manifest for your good. Then, all of a sudden, there's a break because your conversation became perverted. You stop what God is doing in your life. This is why you may not see God moving in certain areas of your life. Your conversation was like a knife that cut you away from the Spirit of God. In order for you to become as He is, you must begin to embrace what He says.

The heart of him that hath understanding seeketh knowledge: but the mouth of fools feedeth on foolishness (Proverbs 15:14).

Check out this kind of conversation: "Did you see his chest? He's got the kind of lips I want to just kiss on all night. Man, I wish I could hit that. Oh, I wish I could rock that." You know you know what I'm talking about. You're just setting yourself up to become best friends with Timothy McVeigh because, if you ain't careful, a whole side of your walk with God will be blown away like that government building in Oklahoma—and that was horrifying!

∞

DON'T BE DECEIVED: AS CUTE AS HE
IS OR AS FINE AS SHE MAY BE, THEY
AIN'T THE EIGHTH WONDER OF
THE WORLD.

∞

The Word is filled with advice about your conversation:

Pleasant words are as an honeycomb, sweet to the soul, and health to the bones (Proverbs 16:24).

A man's belly shall be satisfied with the fruit of his mouth; and with the increase of his lips shall he be filled. Death and life are in the power of the tongue: and they that love it shall eat the fruit thereof (Proverbs 18:20-21).

Better is the poor that walketh in his integrity, than he that is perverse in his lips, and is a fool (Proverbs 19:1).

Hear the right, O Lord, attend unto my cry, give ear unto my prayer, that goeth not out of feigned lips. Let my sentence come forth from Thy presence; let Thine eyes behold the things that are equal. Thou hast proved mine heart; Thou hast visited me in the night; Thou hast tried me, and shalt find

203

nothing; I am purposed that my mouth shall not transgress. Concerning the works of men, by the word of Thy lips I have kept me from the paths of the destroyer. Hold up my goings in Thy paths, that my footsteps slip not (Psalms 17:1-5).

It's plain and simple; when you keep your conversation holy, your feet will not slip.

What Goes in Comes out

We have a lower nature that is influenced by the spirit of this world. I want to give you a revelation from the Word that will set you free. You're getting ready to realize that you are what the Word says you are. Your days of being subjected to the enemy and the tactics of this world are over. From this day forward, you will know that if you are enslaved, it's because you want to be and not because you have to be.

❧

FROM THIS DAY FORWARD, YOU WILL KNOW THAT IF YOU ARE ENSLAVED, IT'S BECAUSE YOU WANT TO BE, NOT BECAUSE YOU HAVE TO BE.

❧

Proverbs 4:20-27 says:

My son, attend to My words; incline thine ear unto My sayings. Let them not depart from thine eyes; keep them in the midst of thine heart. For they are life unto those that find them, and health to all their flesh. Keep thy heart with all diligence; for out of it are the issues of life. Put away from thee a froward mouth, and perverse lips put far from thee. Let thine eyes look right on, and let thine eyelids look straight before thee. Ponder the path of thy feet, and let all thy ways be established. Turn not to the right hand nor to the left: remove thy foot from evil.

You have to *guard* what enters into your eyes and ears and definitely what comes out of your mouth! If you allow satanic things to enter into your ears and your eyes, you may not have actually performed the act, but it will influence you to operate according to what you have seen and heard.

∞

GUARD YOUR HEART. WHEN THE ENEMY CAN'T USE A PERSON TO SEDUCE YOU PHYSICALLY, HE TRIES TO SEDUCE YOU MENTALLY, THROUGH WHAT YOU HEAR AND SEE.

∞

Remember, if the enemy can't bring a person to seduce you, he will still seduce you by what you hear and what you look at. If you want to recover from that sickness, you have to incline your ear to the Word of God. If what you hear and see is coming from the Word, then it will keep you. Words are powerful.

When you play around by saying things like "I sure would like to be with him," the enemy will get a hold of your joke and turn it into reality. That will lead your spirit down the wrong path and cause you to fall into sexual sin. Don't have wandering eyes.

∞

DON'T JOKE AROUND AND SAY, "I SURE WOULD LIKE TO BE WITH HIM." THE ENEMY WILL GET A HOLD OF YOUR JOKE AND TURN IT INTO A REALITY.

∞

Now let's step back for a minute. One of the reasons the spirit of perversion enters in during masturbation is that masturbation goes against the natural law of God. That spirit will speak out through you saying, "I don't need a man. I don't need a woman. I'm alright by myself."

In my own experience and in talking to other people, I have come to the conclusion that masturbating has no spiritual purpose. I believe that when a woman masturbates, she is saying within herself, "I can do without the Adam." When a man masturbates, he is saying, "I really don't need an Eve." When a male and female refuse to be joined together, they are erasing the natural institution of God.

One important fact about masturbation is that masturbating does not produce seed, it spills seed.

Remember when Onan offended God:

And Judah said unto Onan, Go in unto thy brother's wife, and marry her, and raise up seed to thy brother. And Onan knew that the seed should not be his; and it came to pass, when he went in unto his brother's wife, that he spilled it on the ground, lest that he should give seed to his brother. And the thing which he did displeased the Lord: wherefore He slew him also (Genesis 38:8-10).

How Far Are You Willing to Go?

Masturbation has no purpose other than to allow the mental and spiritual seats of your conscience to explore unfamiliar territory. This is how we encounter other spirits that are not like God. In order for you to think correctly, your mind has to be transformed back to the correct state.

I feel that I need to say it one more time, for the record: I believe that what's wrong with masturbation is where the mind has to travel to in order to reach climax. Your mind has to walk down some dark holes and dig up some mess that is supposed to be thrown into the sea of forgetfulness. You actually have to defy the law of God—to work against what God has done in your life—to reach an orgasm.

Since God has separated your sins from you as far as the east is from the west, you had to put on some Nikes to go jogging through the corridors of your mind to get that climax.

I know! I know! Pick your brains up because mine is slapped out, too!

It was at this point when it really hit me hard: "I am going to have to live saved for real!" I mean saved, saved, saved, through and through.

I used to say, "Lord, when I get married, I want him to look like this, dress like this, and act like that. I want him to be tall, with this complexion, and with this hair texture." Does that sound familiar? Ha! Ha! OK now! When I realized that there should be no sex before marriage—and no masturbation, either—I had second thoughts. I said, "Come on in, Jesus, and fix me!"

I was walking in downtown New York when I saw a homeless man and said, "Lord, is that him? Ha! Ha! Lord, just send him. If he's missing a tooth, we'll get him a partial. If he wears thick glasses, we'll get him some contacts. If his one eye is cocked to the left, I'll just stand, sit, and walk to the left of him. People will always think he's looking at me. Ha! Ha! Lord, just purify him. Let him have a job and a sweet spirit and I can deal with the rest. I cannot stay single for the rest of my life. I changed my mind. Just send me Your will and send him soon. *Please!* Ha! Ha!"

Chapter Ten

Kill the Chief

This is where I would like to refer back to leadership because submission has become such a problem in our everyday lives. We have not yet been able to recognize, even as single people, the power of our leadership. For more information on this, I highly recommend a little book the Lord gave me to do some time ago titled *My Inheritance.*

We need to understand that there are three responsibilities based on three different entities: personal responsibility, pastoral responsibility, and God's responsibility. God would never assume our responsibilities, and we could never handle His responsibilities. Neither can we handle the responsibilities of our pastors, or they ours.

Now, I honestly believe that, in combination, all three bring about complete deliverance for an individual who is trying to walk out of sexual sin. What brought me to that conclusion is this: Of all the times that I struggled on my own to walk that thing out—when I didn't have a shepherd protecting me—I failed. It is a known fact that after a sheep walks so many feet away from his shepherd, he's immediately blind. The Bible constantly refers back to that fact.

The Lord is my shepherd; I shall not want. He maketh me to lie down in green pastures: He leadeth me beside the still waters. He restoreth my soul: He leadeth me in the paths of righteousness for His name's sake. Yea, though I walk through the valley of the shadow of death, I will fear no evil: for Thou art with me; Thy rod and Thy staff they comfort me (Psalms 23:1-4).

Now the same nature that God the Shepherd has, the pastor as shepherd has. If the pastor you are now sitting under cannot lead you beside still waters, restore your soul, and help you fear no evil when you walk through a valley experience, there is a problem.

All Three Sectors

Turn your Bible right now to Joshua 10. I would like for you to read the whole chapter because you need to know the full story to get the gist of what happened in the end. In this passage, you will see all three areas of responsibility. You will see the personal call; you will see God helping you in what you're called to do; then, you will see the job of the leader.

I'll use The Living Bible for this chapter:

When Adoni-zedek, the king of Jerusalem, heard how Joshua had captured and destroyed Ai and had killed its king, the same as he had done at Jericho, and how the people of Gibeon had made peace with Israel and were now their allies, he was very frightened. For Gibeon was a great city—as great as the royal cities and much larger than Ai—and its men were known as hard fighters. So King

Adoni-zedek of Jerusalem sent messengers to several other kings: King Hoham of Hebron, King Piram of Jarmuth, King Japhia of Lachish, King Debir of Eglon. "Come and help me destroy Gibeon," he urged them, "for they have made peace with Joshua and the people of Israel." So these five Amorite kings combined their armies for a united attack on Gibeon (Joshua 10:1-5 TLB).

See, this is what happens when the enemy knows that you are about to forsake your old lifestyle. He doesn't just attack you alone. He'll grab every force at his disposal to help him. Every part of that characteristic of sexual sin will be joined together against you. All of a sudden—he'll bring pornography, illicit sex, inordinate sex—every unnatural sexual activity imaginable will come against you at once. Because the enemy knows that you're getting ready to walk out of his clutches, he actually increases his attack on you to hold you there.

NO MATTER WHAT THE ENEMY BRINGS YOUR WAY, NO MATTER HOW FINE SHE IS, NO MATTER HOW GOOD HE LOOKS—NO MORE SHEETS!

The men of Gibeon hurriedly sent messengers to Joshua at Gilgal. "Come and help your servants!" they demanded. "Come quickly and save us! For all the kings of the Amorites who live in the hills are here with their armies." So Joshua and the Israeli army left Gilgal and went to rescue Gibeon. "Don't be afraid of them," the Lord said to Joshua, "for they are already defeated! I have given them to you to destroy. Not a single one of them will be able to stand up to you" (Joshua 10:6-8 TLB).

Joshua represents pastors and the servants represent those submitted to their leaders. Now, you have to remember that even before your pastor assists you in walking out your deliverance, he must receive for himself a personal word from the Lord concerning your situation. That's what causes a leader to know that he has what it takes to bring you through this battle, this warfare. He's gotten a personal word from the Lord concerning you.

The Lord said to Joshua, "Don't be afraid of them, for they are already defeated!" That's why sometimes you'll see a sense of confidence on your leadership. You'll see that they're not shaken concerning your life and concerning your future. They already know that the enemy coming up against you is already a defeated foe.

The Scripture goes on to say, "Joshua traveled all night from Gilgal and took the enemy armies by surprise."

What's the element of surprise? The enemy doesn't expect you to come out of your situation. He thinks that because you're not as skilled or knowledgeable as you desire to be—in the Word of God, or in intercessory prayer, praise and worship—you're already defeated. He thinks he has the victory.

The surprise element is that you have a pastor whom the Lord has already trained to wage this war. Your pastor has the weapons it takes to sneak up on the enemy. If you've had a problem with submission, then the enemy is not expecting you to have leadership. He's not expecting anybody to be covering you and praying for you. Now, you by yourself may not be able to defend the enemy. But you, being covered in prayer and covered by a shepherd, have already won the battle.

Then the Lord threw them into a panic so that the army of Israel slaughtered great numbers of them at Gibeon and chased the others all the way to Beth-horon and Aze-kah and Makhedah, killing them along the way (Joshua 10:10 TLB).

Did you see that? The verse says, "killing them along the way." The killing of this thing is a process—being submitted to authority, being taught the Word of God, being taught how to pray and how to intercede. It doesn't always happen overnight.

∞

YOU DIDN'T GET INTO THE CONDITION YOU ARE IN OVERNIGHT; IT WILL TAKE MORE THAN JUST AN OVERNIGHT PURGING FOR YOU TO GET OUT.

∞

Your leadership and the congregation that you now sit among—your brothers and sisters—are also trained to help you in this battle. All of you together become a weapon for victory.

The enemy is slaughtered along the way. This means that as they came upon the enemy, they killed them—they slaughtered them all. Just remember, some will be slaughtered on Monday, some on Thursday, some in March, and others in June. The thing to remember is that it is a process. They were killed one by one, but they were *all* killed, eventually.

Now let's go back to the Scripture.

And as the enemy was racing down the hill to Beth'horon, the Lord destroyed them with a great hailstorm that con-tinued all the way to Azekah; in fact, more men died from the hail than by the swords of the Israelis (Joshua 10:11 TLB).

What is God trying to say to you? He's saying that when you proceed to fight in your deliverance—to lock arms with leadership and begin to do battle—then the Spirit of God will take over and begin to destroy some of those demonic elements in the realm of the spirit. Sometimes, you won't have to battle. There's a realm in which the enemy fights that is not touchable, not tangible, and not something that you can hold on to.

Let me put it to you plainly: throwing away the condoms and getting rid of all the pornography are enemies you are killing on contact. After the pastor lays the Word of God in your belly, then these are things he's helping to also destroy on contact.

However, the anointing of God, the breath of God, and the Spirit of God begin to do battle on your behalf *in the Spirit*. They kill enemies that are on their way to attack you again. See, the enemy is being destroyed from three realms—the natural realm, the spiritual realm, and the supernatural realm. The Israelites fought with swords, and they killed on contact. Then the Spirit of the Lord got in the wind and sent a hailstorm. He killed what they could not kill. So there was a mass killing going on.

∽

ALLOW THE ANOINTING OF GOD TO
CLOSE THE DOOR ON EVERY DEAD
RELATIONSHIP YOU'VE EVER HAD.

∽

Matthew 16:19 says that *"whatsoever you bind on earth shall be bound in heaven."* Luke 11:2 also talks about the Kingdom of God coming and the will of God being done on earth *"as it is in Heaven."* So when you begin to kill spiritual enemies on earth, the Holy Spirit begins to kill in the spirit realm. This is your guarantee that the root of that thing is being destroyed.

As the men of Israel were pursuing and harassing the foe, Joshua prayed aloud, "Let the sun stand still over Gibeon, and let the moon stand in its place over the valley of Aijalon!" And the sun and the moon didn't move until the Israeli army had finished the destruction of its enemies! This is described in greater detail in The Book Jashar. So the sun stopped in the heavens and stayed there for almost twenty-four hours! (Joshua 10:12-13 TLB)

When you make the decision to start doing battle and letting your pastor help you to do battle, something will happen in the spirit realm. The Lord will stay the hand of time and actually allow you to recover what you've lost. He will give you time now to regain your life. What He is actually saying is that darkness is not going to come over you and the shadow of death is not going to consume you. In other words, the presence of God is going to shine in your situation until you are completely delivered.

God says, "You ain't gonna die in this mess. I'm going to hold back the sun because in order to fight, you have to be able to see. Where the enemy kills you is in the dark. I'm going to let the light of My Word begin to shine in your spirit until you are *completely* delivered."

You have to recognize how that light got there. Who was responsible for giving you the extra time? You have to know who caused God's hand to move against the elements—to hold back the sun. Who? The pastor! Remember, Joshua prayed.

There had never been such a day before, and there has never been another since, when the Lord stopped the sun and moon—all because of the prayer of one man. But the Lord was fighting for Israel (Joshua 10:14 TLB).

You need to know that the Lord is fighting for you! You need to know that while you're discouraged *and* you're feeling like,

"Man, I done messed up." There is somebody else who is fighting for you. The Lord is fighting for you.

(Afterwards Joshua and the Israeli army returned to Gilgal.) During the battle the five kings escaped and hid in a cave at Makkedah. When the news was brought to Joshua that they had been found, he issued a command that a great stone be rolled against the mouth of the cave and that guards be placed there to keep the kings inside. Then Joshua commanded the rest of the army, "Go on chasing the enemy and cut them down from the rear. Don't let them get back to their cities, for the Lord will help you to completely destroy them" (Joshua 10:15-19 TLB).

∞

WHEN WE TRULY ENTER INTO
WORSHIP IN THE SPIRIT, THE SPIRIT
OF GOD LITERALLY DRIVES OUT THE
HORDES OF THE DEVIL.

∞

Remember when I said that there's a responsibility for you? Your job is to keep chasing the enemy. Your job is to keep doing battle with the enemy. Chase that thing—that spirit of pornography, that spirit of illicit sex—and don't let it return. That's the only job that you have to do.

Get rid of everything in your house and around your possessions that represents illegal activity, and don't let it back in your house. Again, that's all your job is. Keep it from returning to the place from which you've chased it.

So Joshua and the Israeli army continued the slaughter and wiped out the five armies except for a tiny remnant that managed to reach their fortified cities. Then the Israelis returned to their camp at Makkedah without having lost a single man! And after that no one dared to attack Israel (Joshua 10:20-21 TLB).

When the enemy sees you fighting like that, he knows what kind of power is fighting with you. The enemy realizes that you have a pastor and the heavenly hosts backing you up, and he doesn't dare fight against you again.

Now these next verses make a very important point. You must look carefully at Joshua 10:22-24:

Joshua now instructed his men to remove the stone from the mouth of the cave and to bring out the five kings—of Jerusalem, Hebron, Jarmuth, Lachish, and Eglon. Joshua told the captains of his army to put their feet on the kings' necks (TLB).

Now you have to understand what's going on here. Let's say you are going through a change—because you tongue-kissed somebody and you became overwhelmed because of it—and you asked God for forgiveness. But, you go back and tongue-kiss that person again and you ask God to forgive you, again. You must understand why you are constantly falling into this same activity. The tongue-kiss is not the chief; it's not the captain. *It's only a symptom of the true spirit,* which is lust.

Do you see that? The spirit of lust is the captain, the chief. If you don't destroy this spirit of lust when you repent, then the same chief will go back, form another army, regroup, and come back again. He is a captain and captains are trained to form armies. This is why you must kill the chief.

OK, now that you've repented for tongue-kissing, you've gotten the pornography out of your house, you've cut off HBO and the sex channels, you have done your part! Now your pastor says, "Let me begin to pray, intercede, and preach the Gospel under the kind of anointing that will destroy the chief."

Remember, you're a member of the Body; there are elders within every congregation. James 5:14 teaches us to call for the elders of the church. The elders will place their feet in prayer on the neck of that chief.

> *"Don't ever be afraid or discouraged," Joshua said to his men. "Be strong and courageous, for the Lord is going to do this to all of your enemies." With that, Joshua plunged his sword into each of the five kings, killing them. He then hanged them on five trees until evening. As the sun was going down, Joshua instructed that their bodies be taken down and thrown into the cave where they had been hiding; and a great pile of stones was placed at the mouth of the cave (The pile is still there today.)* (Joshua 10:25-27 TLB).

Now, what God is saying in this whole passage is that there are three phases of deliverance from every spirit. The first phrase is when you get rid of a portion. The second phase is when you take your situation to someone in authority in your church. They pray over it and then take it to the pastor. The third phase is when the pastor kills the chief.

∾

DON'T GIVE UP. HE WHO BEGAN A
GOOD WORK IN YOU WILL CARRY
IT OUT.

∾

Why do we have repeat offenses? Why are we repeat offenders? Because no one is following the steps and the process to the complete deliverance from this thing. That's the reason there are elders in the Church. This is why the elders of the Church should be purged—to become trustworthy in order to hold in confidence such information. Remember, the chief is murdered from leadership.

So, *if* this process is followed, then I can almost guarantee you that you will be able to walk in freedom. If you open up the door for this spirit to return, then you must walk through the process of deliverance again and again. Who's counting? God certainly isn't. Go back as often as you need to.

❧

WHENEVER YOU CLAIM DELIVERANCE, YOU'D BETTER BE READY TO BE CONFRONTED IN THAT AREA.

❧

When I got submitted to leadership, my ministry went to the nations. People started seeing the evidence of God on my life because my pastor was laying a foundation in my spirit. There was a triple fight going on. I was fighting, my pastor was fighting for me, and the Word was fighting in me. I was being cleansed by the Word.

Now ye are clean through the word which I have spoken unto you (John 15:3).

CHAPTER ELEVEN

The Proverbs 31 Woman

We are not married because we are *not single*. Every time I see a Scripture in the Bible about being single, it only talks about being single in heart. What is God trying to tell us? If you expect God to bring a mate to you, you must get purged of certain ideas: "I'm looking for a mate to satisfy all of my needs. I'm on welfare now, but when my husband comes, he's going to change all that. I'm impressed by all the things this man has—all the things he can buy me."

∞

HAVE YOU EVER WONDERED WHY
YOU'RE NOT MARRIED? YOU'RE
NOT MARRIED BECAUSE YOU'RE NOT
SINGLE YET.

∞

Buy your own furniture, flowers, television, DVD, and car. Then, when he comes, you will be able to make a conscious decision about his character. You won't allow what he has to blind you to the man he really is. This will leave you with enough room to make the right decision.

Women, it is high time that you realize that sheets are expensive. They will cost you your mind. The mind of a powerful woman is a terrible thing to waste. You've got to be busy at your goals. If you are a woman who has not yet set goals for yourself, or if you don't know what road to take, then any road will do. You have to have goals so that you can occupy yourself with your dreams.

As women, we make the mistake of not looking for people who can satisfy us where we are going. We look for people who can satisfy us now. Many marriages are not good because they may be good for now, but may not be good for your future. Can you grow with him? Can he go where you are going in the Spirit? Can you go where he is going in the Spirit?

∞

MANY PEOPLE CHOOSE A MATE WHO CAN ROCK THEIR WORLD RIGHT NOW. GOD WILL CHOOSE A MATE WHO CAN SATISFY WHERE YOU'RE GOING.

∞

That's why the Holy Ghost must lead you. Jesus is Alpha and Omega, the Beginning and the End. He's already at your end before you get there. Let His Holy Spirit lead you because He knows what is down the road. He already knows what you can and cannot take.

We have to have the sense of an eagle. When a female eagle chooses a mate, she takes a branch about the size of her children, flies high in the sky, and drops the branch. The male eagle has to swoop down and catch the branch before it hits the ground and bring it back to her. She says, "You did well that time," and does it a couple more times.

Then she goes and gets a branch *her* same size and flies as high as she possibly can and drops it. She says, "If you can catch this branch that is my size, and you can catch the branch that is the weight of my child, then I know that if anything were to ever happen to me or my children, you would be able to catch us."

We often marry people who can give us good sex, but can't catch us in the Spirit. That's why sex before marriage becomes dangerous—your nose gets opened before your spirit does. Your nose takes control before the anointing takes control, and when that happens, it's too powerful to make a sound decision. So you make a decision out of your flesh and not out of your spirit.

❧

IF WE ALLOWED GOD TO BE OUR
MATCHMAKER, THERE WOULD BE
LESS DIVORCE, MORE COMPATIBILITY,
AND GREATER FULFILLMENT OF HIS
PURPOSES ON THE EARTH.

❧

Where Are You Going?

My sister, your closet, your house, and everything about you should exemplify where you are going and not where you have been. We dress to attract the attention of the man, so he has to see an appearance of where we're going.

Make your home look like a woman of God lives there. Take out the objects that remind you of your worldly past. Worldly outfits tell where you are going or where you have been; get rid of them. Your spirit may be in your future, but if you are still hanging on to those outfits, then your wardrobe is from your past. From your head to your toes, everything should line up with where you are going. Otherwise, you are in a state of confusion.

> *For where envying and strife is, there is confusion and every evil work* (James 3:16).

Women, God is setting you up. He is getting you ready. Your best days are ahead of you. Your worst days are over. As Bishop T.D. Jakes says, "Tell the devil, 'I changed my mind.'" Tell the devil, *"There will be no more sheets!"*

Regardless of how you look, your spirit will tell the story. It takes God to work character in us. We lost character while hanging on the streets outside of the will of God. The Bible says in Proverbs 31:10, *"Who can find a virtuous woman? for her price is far above rubies."*

Do you remember the definition of virtue, to exercise righteousness and moral goodness? I'd like to add this: The exercising of virtue is a necessary ingredient in our walk of faith. Again, who can find a virtuous woman? I have discovered that the reason no one can find a virtuous woman is because she is not found, she is made.

Exercise reminds me of a time I was glancing through a "muscle" magazine in which they listed the names of the female winners for the Best Body. I was saying, "Boy, one day, I'm going to have a body like this one or that one." Mind you, I was sitting there at 165 pounds, with a bowl of ice cream in one hand and a pack of Oreo cookies in the other. That's how some of us are.

I remember hiring a personal trainer and one day after working out, I was so sore that I could hardly lie down without being in pain. The next day, I went to the gym and told my trainer, "You must have hurt me." He said, "You have to exercise that muscle until it tears out of its current position. Then, you must work it out and build it up in the new spot."

∞

WE KNOW WHAT IT TAKES TO SHAPE UP OUR BODIES, BUT WE'RE OFTEN CLUELESS WHEN IT COMES TO FORMING OUR CHARACTER.

∞

So when the Bible says a woman of virtue is hard to find, it's because she must start with a repentant heart, then allow God to assist her in tearing away from her old lifestyle and way of doing things. Yes, it will be painful because she has to tear her flesh away from the old things, then build herself up in God.

A woman should apply herself to exercise daily. You can't exercise one day then wait two weeks to exercise again. If you do that, then the muscle will heal in the old spot without giving you the "cut" that you want. You will have to work out while your muscles are sore.

You will have to do the laundry, on top of cooking, on top of housework, and on top of taking care of the children. You will have to practice to be good. You don't become excellent in your household duties, things of God, or with your creditors instantly. You have to work at it. This means that to be excellent in terms of your creditors, you have to tear yourself away from some of those credit cards.

I'm not saying that it will be easy, but the process to change never is. For me, it was emotionally traumatic. The day that I cut up my credit cards, somebody really should have called the ambulance. I shook, jerked, and crumbled to the floor, yelling out loud, "I can't! I can't! How will I ever make it?"

Let me tell you, my first trip to the mall was "drama." All the cute skirts, suits, and blouses developed eyes and mouths. They were winking and blinking like neon signs. They seemed to be speaking out saying, "Why did you cut up the card? You could've taken me home with you." That day, I came out of the mall with one tube of lipstick, one eyeliner pencil, and one big brown bag of depression. Isn't it funny how when you want something new, all of your old clothes begin to look like rags?

Believe me when I tell you, "Boo, it's going to be drama. Boo, it's going to hurt. But Boo, you'll be *free!*"

Her Price

Her price is far above rubies because she pays a price to be a virtuous woman. She pays the price to be above rubies. It doesn't always mean you have to give this woman a lot of jewels. That woman knows that her spirit is more priceless than gold or diamonds. There is nothing that you can give a virtuous woman that can match what she has exercised her spirit to become. In that, she becomes what her God needs and also what a husband needs.

She makes sure that nothing will be needed in her household. The Lord had to teach me this. Many times, we want to be married but we do not know the basics of caring for a household. The Proverbs 31 woman conditions her house never to run out. She's never caught off guard. She is a prepared woman.

You must prepare yourself now. A man can only expect from you what the Scriptures have promised him you should become. As you begin to practice excellence, you will strive to become what the Word says you should be.

❧

WHAT ARE YOU BRINGING TO THE TABLE BESIDES EYELINER AND LIPSTICK?

❧

Any man that is in the Word will be satisfied by what he sees. He will be patient to know that though you may not be perfect, he will see enough godly attributes in you to say, "If I give her a few more years, she will be all that God wants her to be."

Check out Proverbs 31:15: *"She riseth also while it is yet night, and giveth meat to her household, and a portion to her maidens."* Which means, she is not broke; there's money in the bank.

If your finances permit, your desire to maintain a structured home should be to the degree that you would hire help, if need be. Whatever it takes, you must determine to become organized.

Let's look at what verse 16 says: *"She considereth a field, and buyeth it: with the fruit of her hands she planteth a vineyard."* Is anything in your name besides a bunch of credit cards?

By the time you are married, you should own something. You should be able to say, "I bought this house, even though you don't live in it." You can invest in a little $70,000 fixer-upper, remodel it, and rent it out. A Proverbs 31 woman will push herself to own property and, when she gets a man, push him to own property, too.

She watches for bargains. She is not out spending every dime she's got. She's saying, "I don't have to spend this much right now." She helps to conserve what she has.

You may ask, "Why is she addressing this subject this way?" Because remember what I said before? If you are planning to get married and become a wife—instead of a knife—you must stop the drama right now.

I tell you what: if you can walk *this* walk as a single woman, you are going to be "the Bomb"—*booh yaaw!* You are going to blow up!

My little tulips, *if you want to be somebody, and if you want to go somewhere, you had better wake up and pay attention.*

∞

HOW CAN YOU GET MARRIED WHEN YOU'RE STILL IN DEBT AND CAN'T PAY YOUR BILLS? YOU'RE TOO NEEDY! YOU'RE SUPPOSED TO BE A HELPMEET, NOT A DEADBEAT!

∞

The Present Season

She is not afraid of the snow for her household: for all of her household are clothed with scarlet. She maketh herself coverings of tapestry; her clothing is silk and purple (Proverbs 31:21-22).

Everything in your house, including your wardrobe, should be changed according to the season. You should change the fragrance of the potpourri in your home so that they reflect the season. For example, acorns and chestnuts are things that smell like fall. It also is good for you to change your bed linens so that the patterns and colors represent the change of seasons.

Why am I saying this? Because I do it and it organizes my mind. You may ask yourself, "Why is this important?" It is important because we must flow with the seasons. Now you know, the seasons are going to come around whether you are prepared or not. Why not flow with what God is doing?

The winter months say that it's time to settle, prepare, and think about where I'm going. The spring says it's time to plant and to sow. Remember, if you don't plant anything you will not reap anything. Summer says I am enjoying the fruit of my labor. Yet, I am preparing to be able to enjoy the fruit of my harvest. The fall says I am gathering in my harvest, and this is an important season. As a matter of fact, it is my favorite season because I see the harvest of the seeds I planted in the spring.

> *To every thing there is a season, and a time to every purpose under the heaven...* (Ecclesiastes 3:1).

Remember this: Your mind and your spirit must stay within the *realm of that season.* If you ignore a season, a season can kill you. The first law to success is that you must learn to respect the season. For example, if a person walks outside in the dead of winter wearing sandals, hot pants, and a halter top—and remains outside—that person will surely die.

This is the reason many people have not benefited from life; they do the right thing in the wrong season. Many people in Christendom have become disillusioned by the "bless me" message; they're looking for a blessing for which they have not sown. Galatians 6:7 says, *"Be not deceived; God is not mocked: for whatsoever a man soweth, that shall he also reap."*

Don't tell me that your life won't be different behind that revelation. The Bible says that Isaac sowed in a time of famine and reaped in the same year (see Gen. 26:1,12). Get it? It was in the same year because the seasons were designed to work with nature and not against it.

Anytime there is a force that goes against nature, you will have natural disaster—hurricanes, tornadoes, etc. The temperature from another season has dropped in a present season at the wrong time. Does that sound like you? Now in the form of ebonics, "I be trying to help you." So let's move on.

If nothing else, you must learn to discern the season. Stop right now and ask yourself, "What season am I in?" This is your first step in correcting emotional confusion. It's as simple as this: Take your emotions and set them inside the season. Instantly, they will line up and order will come. You don't have to be led away by emotional turmoil. You can decide what state your emotions will stay in. You are experiencing a tornado. You are operating in the wrong emotions—in the wrong season.

So, whatever time it is when you are reading this book, line your household up with the season you are in now. For example, in the natural, if you bought the book in November, go in the closet and box up summer things. Keep your house in season.

In your spirit woman, look at what you have accomplished in your character up to this point, and if it's not much in comparison to two or three years ago, then this is the time to make the decision to make steps to change your character. You don't have to be under scrutiny from another person's opinions about who you are. Like the turning of the color of leaves in the fall, you will be the first to know and see it. Let's move on.

Strength and honour are her clothing; and she shall rejoice in time to come. She openeth her mouth with wisdom; and in her tongue is the law of kindness (Proverbs 31:25-26).

She is a woman of respect and dignity. She's not a loudmouthed, disrespectful woman who is constantly "going off." She handles everything with the utmost sense of grace. She is a lady at all times. She has strength; therefore, she is not easily flustered by anything and everything.

When she speaks, she is kind. The Lord has taught me to never speak in the heat of the battle. Always wait until the cool of the day. If you can't allow others to know they have offended you without hurting them, then you have inflicted pain while trying to get your pain relieved, and that's not the way of the Lord. Kindness is a rule. This means she makes it a point to be kind.

> *She looketh well to the ways of her household, and eateth not the bread of idleness.... Favour is deceitful, and beauty is vain: but a woman that feareth the Lord, she shall be praised* (Proverbs 31:27,30).

She does not fear age. If she has kept herself in honesty and dignity, the Lord is going to preserve her. Have you noticed that sin ages you? God will allow you to enjoy your life to the point at which every year becomes a valuable year to you. Therefore, you won't begrudge age. She is not 50 years old, wearing teenagers' clothes still trying to be 15.

We who are single should be governing our lives, as single women, to strive to become women who can be praised. Many women feel that they can get a man simply because they have a nice body and a pretty face; that may be true, but none of those things help to build a house.

❦

HOW CAN YOU EVEN THINK ABOUT
GETTING MARRIED WHEN YOU DON'T
KNOW HOW TO COOK, CAN'T WASH
CLOTHES, AND YOUR HOUSE IS
ALWAYS TORN UP?

❦

This brings me to the story of Esther and Vashti. In Esther chapter 1, we learn that Vashti was gorgeous and she had the kingdom at her disposal. One day, the king declared a feast and he called her out so that the people could behold her beauty, but Vashti disrespected him by not coming out (see Esther 1:12).

This story goes to show you that beauty is only skin-deep. As beautiful as Vashti was, when she disrespected the king, she lost her inheritance. Her character had not been constructed to perform the duties of a queen. Surely her shape was palace material, but her character was designed for the pits.

∞

YOUR SEXY SHAPE WILL NOT DETERMINE YOUR LEVEL OF BLESSING. GOD IS GOING TO BLESS YOU ACCORDING TO YOUR LEVEL OF INTEGRITY.

∞

Esther was not only beautiful, but she had been preparing herself for an entire year (see Esther 2). She had a goal. You have to approach life that way. You have to be prepared, and your attitude should be, "I'm going to see what I can do for God. What can I do for my people?" She knew that when she went before the king, she had a purpose.

Any woman who is striving for character perfection must do so with a goal and purpose in mind. You have to ask yourself, "What good can I do for the Kingdom of God if I be joined with a man?"

We need to know what to look for in a man. Proverbs 4:7 in The Living Bible says, *"Getting wisdom is the most important thing you can do! And with your wisdom, develop common sense and good judgment."* If the man has no sense and his words are not full of the wisdom of God, then run from him.

But many of us are so caught up in the natural things—"He is so fine. I just love the way he talks to me. He makes me feel wonderful." These are not reasons, nor are they foundations or guarantees to a successful marriage.

Girlfriend, before you start looking for qualities in a man, build some qualities in yourself. Here are just a few that I think need to be addressed:

1. Be Accountable

I have a beautiful home that I can afford to live in alone. However, I have chosen for people to live with me. When I come into the house at 3:00 A.M. and it's not a church night, I need for someone to know where I've been. My mother used to say, "After midnight, ain't nothing open but legs." In the wee hours of the morning, if you are not already in trouble, you are about to get in trouble.

∽

AFTER MIDNIGHT, AIN'T NOTHING
OPEN BUT LEGS!

∽

If you are accountable to someone, then you are less likely to be mindless in these situations. You will be more likely to think about the consequences of your actions.

2. Get out of Debt

There will always be a sale. Women are always trying to be divas—wearing clothes that they can't afford, trying to be glamorous on credit. You can't be a diva for Jesus. You have to drop that worldly spirit. You have to rid yourself of that residue. You must allow God to purge your spirit and your wardrobe.

Women go into debt because of the internal conflict they face. We have to constantly buy things to make us feel better about ourselves. There's not an outfit you can buy that can cleanse your soul from sexual sin—that's God's job. You are trying to pacify yourself with things when your real problem is sin-sickness. Only God can heal that.

Nothing can drive you out of the will of God. Remember, we are carried away by our own lusts. We are not carried away with the lust that someone else brings us. We are carried away by the lust that we allow to infiltrate our own spirits. Those of you who are in debt need to cut up your credit cards. Realize that you cannot buy your way out of sexual impurity.

The Bible says you should desire integrity above riches. I would rather have two blouses and one skirt from Kmart that I wear to church, knowing that my spirit is clean and that I have peace of mind, than to have all the clothes in the world—and a beauty shop appointment twice a week—and have no peace.

3. Be Disciplined

Once you let an ungodly spirit into your life, it will attempt to take over your entire life. If you become undisciplined in washing the dishes, the next thing you know, you will become undisciplined in going to the cleaners, then undisciplined in taking a bath, then you may become undisciplined in cleaning the house, then in the way you pay your bills. Once a door opens, it eats like a cancer until it eats up all that's good in you. Pretty soon, you may not have discipline in anything. You are just a wild buck.

Those of us who are undisciplined need to start today by saying, "There is something that I'm going to start doing now. I declare that every day at this time, this is what I am going to do." Prayer would be an excellent place to start. That is the way you break that spirit of being undisciplined.

∞

GOD IS CALLING US TO PRAYER, CONSECRATION, AND SANCTIFICATION.

∞

The reason your sexual life is out of order is because an *undisciplined person never says, "enough."* An undisciplined person will say I want it when I want, how I want it, as many times as I want, and with as many people as I want to do it with. The majority of undisciplined acts are in direct violation of the Word of God.

When you become disciplined in all areas of your life—praying, controlling your spending habits, being on time for church—you are teaching your flesh that it can't have its way every day. You will say to your flesh, "You do it this way now *because my spirit rules. The anointing that's in me rules my flesh!*"

When you start being disciplined, then the next time you are confronted with a sexual temptation, it won't be as hard to tell your flesh, "No," because your flesh is already used to hearing that. Your flesh will say, "I know you're going to say, 'No.'" That's called discipline.

If you can't control your flesh—when that spirit of sloth is telling you to oversleep and be late for work, or don't pay your bills on time, or don't walk in integrity—then the same spirit will approach you with sexual sin. You have to understand that it's all a sin before God. All sin is sin to God. The difference with

235

sexual sin is that it leaves another spirit—a tormenting spirit—in you. Now let's go on and add some more layers, Boo.

∽

WHEN YOU DISCIPLINE YOURSELF,
YOUR SPIRIT RULES YOUR FLESH.

∽

4. Develop Character

When you are undisciplined, it will affect your character. It will affect the way you speak to people and whether or not you respect people. People without character will say anything. They don't keep their word.

People who don't have character don't know how to properly judge character. When the majority of the people you have slept with have no character, then you have to realize that you attract your own kind. Sometimes we get treated like dogs because we have treated ourselves like dogs. Dogs always run with other dogs. No matter what the type is, a dog knows a dog. The Word tells us:

> So now you can look forward soberly and intelligently to more of God's kindness to you when Jesus Christ returns. Obey God because you are His children; don't slip back into your old ways—doing evil because you knew no better. But be holy now in everything you do, just as the Lord is holy, who invited you to be His child. He Himself has said, "You must be holy, for I am holy" (1 Peter 1:13-16 TLB).

∽

DON'T EVEN THINK ABOUT SLIPPING
BACK INTO YOUR OLD WAYS—YOU
KNOW BETTER.

∽

Seeing in the Right Light

When you have constructed your life—gotten your character in order and have self-respect—then you must begin to control the way in which a man treats you and the way you treat yourself. For example, when a man invites you out on a date nowadays, I believe that the safest date is breakfast.

Breakfast says, "It's early in the relationship." Candlelight and nighttime meals hide and conceal the windows of your heart: your eyes. If you look into a person's eyes, you can see right into their spirit. When you've been purged and cleansed and have a discerning spirit, then you can immediately recognize someone without character. You can't see that in candlelight, at night, in a dark restaurant.

The devil always casts a shadow on what he does. When you go to breakfast with a man, the sun is brightly shining. Everything about him is wide open. You are more alert in the morning. You don't have a strong sex drive then. You are able to look at that man and have a conversation. You will be able to see if he is wise and knowledgeable. By evening time, your guard is down. When night falls, it's time to go to bed.

Breakfast says, "It's time to wake up and smell the coffee." Lunch says, "I want a little bit more to eat, but I need just a little more daylight than evening." Just as Joshua prayed during the battle we read about in the last chapter, you can say, "Lord, I can win this war if You just give me a little more daylight." That's what a lot of women need to say, "Lord, I can make the right decision. I can see what I need to see, but I need a little bit more daylight." That's when God will bring lunchtime.

By the time you accept an evening dinner, you're saying, "I've been awake and alert. I've seen him in the Spirit. I've heard his conversation. I've had enough daylight to judge his spirit and his character, and I think there's a future here. It's late in the relationship. It's time for us to make some decisions."

When that dinner comes, marriage should be discussed. Even though it's nighttime, I've seen in the daytime what I need to see in his spirit. I know that if I can trust what I've seen in the daytime, then I can trust him when I lay down at night. I know I'm protected in the dark because he is my covering.

Women are receptors and men are projectors. When it's all said and done—when you finish bedding down a man—you are the one whose spirit will be loaded. There is a penalty that men pay for projecting; but the penalty for a woman falsely receiving is that *you* will have to carry the spirit of the act committed.

Did you just understand what you just read? You have to control how a man treats you! Now here comes the next and final level: One of the reasons we err in our judgment and our actions on dates is because we have nothing to compare our right or wrong to. Now, before you make the decision to begin embracing your new lifestyle, I'm going to list a few "do's" and "don'ts" for your dating pleasure.

Oh, you thought this was just another book? *Bong!* Wrong answer! This is a new way of life for you!

1. Never start talking about marriage on the first seven dates.

2. If someone for whom you have a strong attraction (or vice versa), invites you to an evening event, make it a group thing.

3. Never sit at home idle, waiting for him to call you.

4. Allow him to pursue you. Remember that a real man will.

5. Always keep your first seven dates filled with educational and cultural things. It helps to stimulate the intellect and not the sex drive.

6. If he comes to take you out and it's past 9:30 P.M., don't go, because you know what he came for—and it's not for your knowledge of the Word. That's a call, girlfriend, and you know what kind of call it is—a booty call.

7. Allow a man to be a man in every sense of the word. Do not start out with that "let me help you" spirit. Allow him to flourish in his own masculinity by opening doors, paying the check.

8. While at the breakfast, lunch, or dinner table, you tell him what you want on the menu and allow him to order for both of you. It's also a way for him to get his respect.

9. Do not allow a potential mate to call your house after midnight, especially while lying in bed. Reclining brings on a different aura. Sit up and stay focused. If he chooses to call after midnight, then tell him to call back at 8 or 9 A.M. Let that be your morning conversation. Everyone knows you are more focused in the morning.

10. Never allow a man to blow his horn for you. Let him come to your door, ask for you properly, and escort you to the car. Anything could happen to you while coming out of the house. You need to feel like he's your protector.

11. Returning home from a date is a crucial time. The added pressure against you is the fact that you just fed

the flesh; it is sluggish and off guard. Be careful not to become too touchy feely and "sloppy agape." He does not have to come into your house. Just because he bought dinner doesn't mean you owe him a kiss, a pat, or a feel. All you owe him is a "Thank you!"

12. Don't allow a man to call you pet names early in the relationship. It is a form of dismantling your posture to become too common too soon!

13. Do not allow any man to indulge in a sexual conversation on your first seven dates—like constantly making comments about the way you are built. That's called *the big hype-up to lay you down!*

14. On first dates, dress conservatively because, remember, the attention must not be drawn to any part of your physical body. When you dress naked, you leave nothing to the imagination and you cause him to never tap into the real person you are!

∞

WHEN A NO-GOOD DEMON SAYS, "HEY, BABY, I SURE WOULD LIKE TO GET WITH YOU," THEN YOU SHOULD EXAMINE THE WAY YOU LOOK AND DRESS.

∞

15. Always insist on his meeting your family and friends. Any man who starts out by turning you away from your friends may have ulterior motives. He's setting you up for the big kill, and there will be no one there for you to fall back on!

16. If you are very serious about your interest in a person, before there is any talk of marriage, always insist that he meet your pastor—shepherds can see farther than the sheep can. I can remember times when I've brought a man I liked to my pastor. He would get this look on his face, shake his hand, and say, "Come back and see us sometime." I knew right then, pastor was saying, "Don't ever bring him back anymore." I have done that so much until I'm tired of bringing people to him, so I decided to give him a break. There should be a one- to three-year distance between relationships. I believe that it is safe to wait as I did. I don't believe that you should date someone when you've not completely healed from the last relationship. Combining the two can only prove to be detrimental to a possibly good relationship.

17. If a man invites you to his home for any reason at all—whether it's to see his trophies or his pet, help him decorate, or even to see the ashtray he made in first grade—always take a friend. Remember, you're walking into his territory, where his spirit rules. That's just like a mouse walking to the throat of a lion's mouth thinking he's going to turn around and walk back out; mind you, the lion hasn't eaten in a while.

18. Men, if a woman invites you to her home and it is early on during your season of dating, it is not unmasculine to say that you wouldn't feel comfortable doing that. The message that you're actually sending is that you're uncomfortable with the idea of being in her home and you think she's pushing this too fast. You've just got your point across without hurting her feelings.

19. Be careful about a man who is uncomfortable giving you his home or personal cell number and asks you to leave messages at his job or a friend's house. Instead of calling you, he's returning your call. Any man who wants to date you and is separated from his wife in the process of being divorced, and he knows within his heart that it's over, still shouldn't get any play until he is completely divorced. This could be an indication that he knows how to settle the emotional aspect of the relationship, but he is incapable of bringing closure to difficult situations.

20. Places to go on the first seven dates should be chosen intelligently and not emotionally. Wonderful places to go are art museums, wholesome Broadway plays, professional sporting events, rollerblading, and horseback riding. If you've never been horseback riding, there's an opportunity for him to take the lead in finding a stable for both of you to learn how to ride. If you choose one of these outings for first dates, I'm almost sure that there will be enough conversation between you to develop a strong bond of compatibility. Where possible, I highly recommend that you go to the play *Phantom of the Opera*. It's a wonderful story about the masked man and the beautiful woman. In all essence, your date may be a masked man, so you really would want to see that one.

21. If it's just a friendship, then on the first two to three dates, the bill should be shared. If he is pursuing you, then the bill should be paid by him.

22. People have asked me questions about flowers. I believe the rose makes much too powerful a statement.

Try and stay away from that flower until there is definitely love involved! If you are going to give flowers to a woman within the first seven dates or the first two months, let it be a bouquet of various flowers. If you're going to give flowers to a man, let it be a "Have a Happy Day" or "Thinking of You" coffee mug with a small bouquet inside the cup. A rose says, "I love you" a bouquet says, "I'm just thinking of you."

23. Never say, "I love you," on the first seven dates. *Never! Never!* How do you know that's good advice? In order for us to learn to love God, we must learn *Him.* So, I'm a firm believer that you don't love a person and you're not in love with a person until you know that person. If you say those powerful three words too soon, then what you're actually saying is, "I love you just the way you are." Therefore, he'll see no reason to change.

24. If you are dating and you have children from a previous relationship, I don't believe that your child needs to be exposed to this man or woman until it has been confirmed and finalized that this is a potential relationship for marriage. In the case of single mothers, there are too many "uncles" in homes today—Uncle Earl, Uncle Charles, Uncle Bill, Uncle Whoever-you-date, especially when you are an only child! During the times that he's picking you up, make sure your child is in a safe and secure place, not having to be constantly exposed to different men running in and out of the child's life. Though you choose to take your life on a roller coaster, your child should never have to be exposed to the drama.

25. Never date a man who even *looked* as if he was going to hit you in the heat of a disagreement—because later on in the relationship, *he will!* If he ever hits you, you better believe that he'll do it again. I don't know about you, but I signed off with whippins' with my father.

26. Never discuss your financial status with a man early on in your relationship. And never, never, never accept money from a man or ask him to assist you in your financial affairs. Remember that he is not Jehovah Jireh, your Provider.

27. And last but not least...you've got to listen up now: remember when I said that men are projectors and women are receptors? When you make a decision to have sex with any man who does not possess godly qualities, you *will* contract something that is deadlier than a disease. Remember, the Bible teaches that when a relationship is consummated, the two shall become one. Therefore, you must be careful as to what spirit is about to step inside of you. I have seen women have nervous breakdowns and even kill themselves behind a deadly relationship. *Now tell me it's only sex!*

Now that we are building a building, shall we proceed to the next floor?

I have designed what I call a Certificate of Accountability on the following page. You must find someone to sign off on this if you are really serious about changing your future! I know you say, "I don't want anybody in my business," but the first step toward staying clean is giving the power of accountability to someone you trust.

You must allow someone else to be honest enough with you to say, "This isn't safe. That's not God. You need to be careful!" I know this looks dumb, but if AA (Alcoholics Anonymous) and NA (Narcotics Anonymous) can be responsible for people they don't know, then we, as brothers and sisters in the Body of Christ, can do the same thing for each other.

So get a pen, pencil, marker, or even blood and tear this vow out and make it! It's not stupid—it's *protection!*

No More Sheets
Certificate of Accountability

Believing that two are better than one, we covenant with each other regarding our dating relationships. We promise to pray with each other before our dates. We will also call each other afterward to ask questions SUCH AS THE FOLLOWING:

Did you stick to your plan for the date?

Did you include others in your activities?

Did you encourage each other?

Did you meet in a safe place?

What time did you get in?

Did you do anything that's not pleasing to God?

What will you do differently next time?

_____

(Signature)

_____

(Signature)

Two are better than one; because they have a good reward for their labor. For if they fall, the one will lift up his fellow: but woe to him that is alone when he falleth; for he hath not another to help him up (Ecclesiastes 4:9-10).

CHAPTER TWELVE

The Other Side of the Gender

There's been so much talk about Adam and Eve in The Garden. What happened? What did Eve do? What did Adam do? I believe that we must begin to place emphasis on the fact that God, through His divine plans, has allowed both males and females to redeem themselves.

Whenever we hear about this story, we think in terms of what Adam should have said and done. But as I walk back through the painful corridors of my mind, no one can really tell you how you should have conducted yourself in any given situation unless they have walked a mile in your shoes.

There are two sides to every story. For example, if I wanted to dismantle or discredit any male, there are enough stories in the Bible to support me. If I wanted to only portray the negative side of the male gender, then I could. Since most of us spend most of our time in the negative, we want to see men as dogs.

However, I found out when I looked back over things that happened to me, there were signs about my character and my personality that said, "Y'all can take advantage of me. Just walk on me. I'm nothing but a rug anyway." There are always warnings before the relationship goes sour.

The enemy works very hard to destroy the masculinity of men. In the beginning, God took a rib from Adam and made Eve. This is why we females cannot deny that our beginning came from the male. I'm a firm believer that part of our womanhood and part of what makes us feel like being women comes from the aura of men.

If the enemy can destroy that—cut off the masculinity and start influencing men to walk and act feminine—it will cause us to be left feeling naked. We'll feel as if we were left without help, without assistance. Actually, in some areas, this may begin to stunt our growth as women.

I don't care what happens or what kind of experience you've had with a man; there is something that lies deep in the depths of the belly of a real woman that is triggered when complemented by a real man. Something happens to you when you're assisted across the street or have a car door opened for you by a man. I don't care what you say, *something* happens in your inner being.

I did not say that all women will be married. But I am saying that on this earth, whether it's for relationship purposes or whether it's for marriage purposes, we cannot do without the male gender. Never give up your right as a woman to need the presence of a man. By rejecting what He made and called good, you defy God, and that offends Him.

The man you were with may have treated you badly, but that's no reason to hate all men. Reject the character of the people who have caused you great pain and harm, but don't reject the gender of the person. When you reject what God has made, that's when it gets dangerous.

Now, as I first stated, there are enough conversations about the negative than we know what to do with. But I believe that in order for that pattern to be broken, there must be someone who will stand up and teach in a new way.

If all a person has been taught is one way of doing something, society bashing them will not change that individual. For example, I have been in direct communication with all of my past relationships except for two. We were able to dialogue and find out what he did and what I did. This was a sign of maturity, sensitivity, respect, and honor. It also gave me insight into what I did not need to repeat in my character.

As I looked back at those times, I found out that I was placing demands on the character of a person who had not come from my background. I entered into the relationship with one set of ideas, and he entered into the relationship with another set. What made it even more complicated was that this was coupled with a physical relationship. Therefore, both parties figure: "Oh well, the sex is good and I love you. You love me, so let's go on."

❧

ANY RELATIONSHIP THAT OFFENDS
THE HOLY SPIRIT IS NOT BIRTHED
THROUGH THE SPIRIT OF GOD.

❧

Now remember, every time you come together with a person, that person is bonding more and more and more with the soulish part of you. Emotions are going wild. However, on the basis of character, expectations, discipline, respect, and being able to satisfy what the individual is desiring out of you, both parties are at a complete loss and are constantly disappointed.

We need to drop this terminology from our lips: Men are dogs. I believe that such terminology offends the very essence of God. He made dogs, and every one of them has four feet and a tail.

∾

Men are not dogs. That terminology offends the very essence of God.

∾

Duplicate Yourself

Great offenses from the other side of the gender come from the lack of true guidance—whether male or female, biological or spiritual. I am saying this because I've seen mothers raise sons and mold them into real men. I have seen young men whose biological fathers had no character—they were alcoholics, drug addicts, you name it—who were fortunate enough to have had other men and women in the church to spend time training them. Those men turned out being nothing like their biological parents.

You see, my brothers, it takes a real, mature man to be able to say to another man, "My brother, I didn't get this right. My character needs help. I really don't know who I am because I have allowed all the women I've been with to define me. I have gained the respect of women in the sheets; now I'm ready for self-respect."

Brothers, I remember noticing something about my biological brother: the older he gets, the more he resembles my dad—both in looks and in character. He is such a gentleman. He opens doors and buys flowers for his wife of five kids.

Watch this: My dad had four girls before he got a son. I guess the Lord was trying his spirit to find out how he would treat us before he got a son. Now, I honestly believe that had my brother come first, we would probably be like peasant damsels in distress. Ha! Ha! Because even now, my brother is the golden child—even though my dad does throw us girls a bone from time to time.

What happened to my brother and his wife when they started a family? They had four girls, and then they got a son. What's so awesome is that my brother treats his girls the way our father treated my sisters and me. He would walk on water for us.

To be honest with you, my sisters and I are spoiled rotten and beyond measure by Dad—even today. So now, I am kind of being de-programmed as we speak. *Please pray for me!* Ha! Ha! I'm not saying that you shouldn't have goals or expectations, but I think ours were a bit much!

In giving you that little background, I just wanted to say that the power of a real man is this—are you ready? Here it is: Men have always been the projectors. Women give birth to what you produce. What causes a child to be born is in your seed. The seed of a child lies in your loins. Therefore, it is already your natural ability to produce.

What did God tell Adam to do? He said, *"Be fruitful and multiply..."* (Gen. 1:22). Now, what does Christ require us to do? Paul said his goal was for Christ to be formed in us (see Gal. 4:19). Christ is constantly after us to look like Him and be like Him. This is the purpose for us being born again. When we come into this world, we are born and shaped in iniquity. Therefore, in order for us to resemble the character of God, we must be born again.

253

What I am saying is that a man has the power to find another brother whom he knows has a misperception of manhood and use his own character and God-given abilities to bring about change in that brother. People are yelling real loud about mentoring, but to mentor means to have the power to transfer your spirit into the life of another.

Just like women have a responsibility to our sisters, men have a responsibility to their brothers. I know you guys can put clothes on—the Armani ties and suits and 'gator shoes—but who have you transferred your thoughts to lately?

If you don't choose to broaden and expand who you are, then when you leave this earth, your earthly life literally is over. But every man who chooses to take a part of your good qualities causes you to live on. There is power in you to duplicate yourself.

You may say, "I don't have a kid." Well ask God to help you find one in a hurry or find another brother to whom you may impart wisdom. This is what is meant by, *"Let brotherly love continue"* (Heb. 13:1).

You Define You

My prayer today for every man reading this chapter is this: Don't ever allow any woman to be your definition. Only choose someone who can add definition. Now that is a very powerful statement!

When you have allowed God to impart wisdom and knowledge within you and you have spent time—I mean quality time—not dating anyone but just working on definition, then you are able to look not *at* a sister, but *within* that sister and see and hear her wisdom. From that (not by how wonderful she looks) you are able to determine whether the character inside the physical shape will fit into your life. If you choose a mate for any other reason than that, you might be getting a knife instead of a wife. The Bible says that you must be sober, meaning not intoxicated, but alert.

❧

TAKE YOUR TIME IN ANY
RELATIONSHIP. ONCE YOU'RE
MARRIED, YOU'LL HAVE THE REST OF
YOUR LIVES TOGETHER. SO MAKE A
WISE CHOICE.

❧

Listen, I also believe that there are some sisters that owe some brothers some apologies. Now why am I saying this? I know you do, because I did. The devil, your adversary, is seeking whom he may devour.

You see, all we have been hearing for the longest is what *he* did. But there are a large number of women whose motives from the get-go were to land a brother who had definition. Some of them spent hundreds of dollars to get your millions. Let me give you a few signs of a gold digger: when a woman begins to become more concerned about your bank book than your expectations, get rid of her as fast as you can.

❧

SOME WOMEN WILL SPEND HUNDREDS
TO GET A MAN'S MILLIONS. IF SHE IS
MORE CONCERNED ABOUT YOUR BANK
BOOK THAN YOUR EXPECTATIONS, GET
RID OF HER AS FAST AS YOU CAN.

❧

Notice small things and simple thoughts in order to see the man and not the things. I believe that has been the downfall of so many potentially good relationships.

I remember going with this guy. He was very nice and he had money. We went to the mall and he wanted to buy me a suit that was very, very expensive, so I kept refusing. Later on, I asked him, "What is behind the nice suit and the money?" I went on to say, "I don't want things; I can buy myself things. I want to know the person."

My brothers, do you know why I am saying this? Remember, marriage is for better or for worse. If you have the right spirit and your integrity and character are correct, and if you were to lose everything, your woman would still stand by you. With those ingredients residing in your person, you can get money again and again and again.

The Bible talks about the fact that when you allow God—and I must repeat this—to purify and purge you, then your discernment will return and you will be able to see what a woman needs. From the very beginning, when you say your marriage vows, you are supposed to be our strength, our protection, and our providers.

I believe that because of a lack of trust, today's women have chosen to work, even when their husbands make good money. Back in the 1950s, the man took on the role of sole provider. You see, my father had such definition until my mom knew that he was going to provide, no matter what.

This is why the wisdom of the matter should be to find someone with as much Proverbs 31 in her as you possibly can, because this woman causes your name to be praised in the gates. If you are going to choose for the future, then you must begin to prepare your physical body as well as your spiritual body right now.

Remember when I said earlier that men are projectors and women are receptors? Then know this: There is a penalty to be paid for wrong projections and misguided erections. The Word declares that when this is done with the idle woman, she takes your strength.

> *Give not thy strength unto women, nor thy ways to that which destroyeth kings* (Proverbs 31:3).

∞

What you lust after determines where you deposit your strength.

∞

The Living Bible refers to this as *"the royal pathway to destruction."*

> *Lust not after her beauty in thine heart; neither let her take thee with her eyelids. For by means of a whorish woman a man is brought to a piece of bread: and the adulteress will hunt for the precious life. Can a man take fire in his bosom, and his clothes not be burned?...But whoso committeth adultery with a woman lacketh understanding: he that doeth it destroyeth his own soul* (Proverbs 6:25-27,32).

The wisdom of the matter is that men have less physical strength after a certain age. This type of excessive physical activity will steal strength and life from your future.

∞

Sex with a woman not your spouse will sap your strength—and eventually you will die. If you're dead to God, you won't fulfill your destiny.

∞

Let's look at the story of Sampson in the Book of Judges:

And the children of Israel did evil again in the sight of the Lord; and the Lord delivered them into the hand of the Philistines forty years. And there was a certain man of Zorah, of the family of the Danites, whose name was Manoah; and his wife was barren, and bare not. And the angel of the Lord appeared unto the woman, and said unto her, Behold now, thou art barren, and barest not: but thou shalt conceive, and bear a son. Now therefore beware, I pray thee, and drink not wine nor strong drink, and eat not any unclean thing: For, lo, thou shalt conceive, and bear a son; and no razor shall come on his head: for the child shall be a Nazarite unto God from the womb: and he shall begin to deliver Israel out of the hand of the Philistines (Judges 13:1-5).

Please notice that the fifth verse states that the child shall be a Nazarite. Nazarites had to follow a strict code of ethics. This means that whatever God has planned for your life, there are certain things that you can and cannot do. Violating those rules tampers with the call of God that is within you.

Understand this: Sampson lost his *insight* long before he actually lost his *eyesight*. When he laid his eyes upon Delilah, he became blinded to the purpose by which he was called. (You should read the entire story in Judges 16.)

Remember when I said earlier that a woman may be your physical desire and your physical type, but her character is deadly to your soul? Look at this man: His future was already mapped out for him. All he had to do was respect the will of God laid out for his life.

When he began to defile himself with Delilah, she was able to seduce him, and it was there that he lost his strength. But, look at the revelation to this story: He had to become incarcerated. What does that mean? He was put in a position where nothing around him mattered to him. He was set in a place where he was forced to commune with the Lord.

Right now, I sense that some of you have had this same experience. You see, when there is a great task ahead of you and you have lost your strength, you must return to the person who strengthened you in the first place. You may ask, "How did blind Sampson get enough strength to kill more in his death than while he was living?" He got in that cell and God gave him *insight*. This is where the secret to your success lies.

You need to have the *power of insight* and not the *lust of eyesight*. When Sampson gained insight, he knew where he went wrong and, at that point, he wanted to kill everything that was against God. The enemy only attacks great men of God with strong, whorish women when he knows that there is greatness within them. That kind of woman kills the purpose of God in you.

> *Hearken unto me now therefore, O ye children, and attend to the words of my mouth. Let not thine heart decline to her ways, go not astray in her paths. For she hath cast down many wounded: yea, many strong men have been slain by her. Her house is the way to hell, going down to the chambers of death* (Proverbs 7:24-27).

When you have recovered your insight, then you can finally recognize who you are, then you will be able to clearly bring yourself back in focus. Only when this happens will you be able to help kill that same mentality in your brothers.

Remember when I said that a woman will spend hundreds to get your millions? That is the spirit of the strange woman, and she doesn't stop there. She will also say whatever she needs to say to seduce you. When her conversation is directed to what's in your pants—and not what's in your heart, your mind, or your spirit—then she is a modern-day Delilah who will strip you.

❧

A MODERN-DAY DELILAH IS A WOMAN WHO IS MORE INTERESTED IN WHAT'S IN YOUR PANTS THAN WHAT IS IN YOUR HEART, MIND, AND SPIRIT.

❧

That's what I call a brother being raped. Yes, she may not be physically strong enough to throw you down on the bed and rape you, but what is worse is that she rapes you of your goals, your purpose, and your strength, and sometimes it's just by her cunning words. Let's look at Proverbs 5:1-6:

> *My son, attend unto my wisdom, and bow thine ear to my understanding: that thou mayest regard discretion, and that thy lips may keep knowledge. For the lips of a strange woman drop as an honeycomb, and her mouth is smoother than oil: but her end is bitter as wormwood, sharp as a two-edged sword. Her feet go down to death; her steps take hold on hell. Lest thou shouldest ponder the path of life, her ways are moveable, that thou canst not know them.*

It is a fact that if you keep losing strength, after awhile, your physical body and your spirit man will become completely dead.

> *The man that wandereth out of the way of understanding shall remain in the congregation of the dead* (Proverbs 21:16).

This is the reason you must take control of your own spirit so that your spirit, along with the Word, will bring clear definition and keep you from constantly being attacked and seduced. Look at this Scripture:

He that hath no rule over his own spirit is like a city that is broken down, and without walls (Proverbs 25:28).

Now when there are no walls to protect a city, any stranger, thief, or murderer can enter into your city (which is your spirit) and destroy it completely. Had I used this Scripture, I would never have married the person I married.

I know men are heavily criticized, but I believe the reason we, as women, have not seen the *brother* in men come out, is because we have been pulling on the flesh. Many of us women have constantly placed a demand on the sexual part and not the brother side. Brothers, by the same token, placed a demand on the sexual side of their relationships with women instead of the sister side.

❦

MEN, LOOK FOR CHARACTER—NOT JUST OUTER BEAUTY. FAR TOO MANY DECISIONS ARE MADE WITH HORMONES INSTEAD OF A HEART SUBMITTED TO GOD.

❦

I know, I know, many of you brothers are saying, "But, Sis, you don't know my nature; it's really high." Well, you must decide whether or not you will walk with a high nature or a holy nature. Listen, I've been there, but I must constantly go back to Second Peter 1:2-4:

Grace and peace be multiplied unto you through the knowledge of God, and of Jesus our Lord, according as His divine power hath given unto us all things that pertain unto life and godliness, through the knowledge of Him that hath called us to glory and virtue: whereby are given unto us exceeding great and precious promises: that by these ye might be partakers of the divine nature, having escaped the corruption that is in the world through lust.

When I read the second verse, I automatically begin to feel better because immediately grace and peace of God begin to settle and cast down my imaginations. I begin to understand that the knowledge of God is more constructive for me than the knowledge of what's going on in my flesh. Then it is up to me to choose the next step. Remember, the power of decision will always be yours. A heavenly host is not going to come and stand around your shoulders and sing, "Hallelujah, hallelujah. Zip up your pants. Hallelujah, hallelujah, don't lay down." That ain't getting ready to happen. Ha! Ha! Ha!

∽

NOT COMMITTING ACTS CONTRARY TO THE WORD OF GOD IS A DECISION. IT WILL BE EASIER TO DECIDE NOW THAN TO DECIDE IN THE FACE OF TEMPTATION.

∽

The Covenant of Rings

Why do you think it was necessary for men to be circumcised? Have you ever really thought about it? Well allow me, if you would, to share this with you. Now, I know right now a lot of you brothers are getting ready to trip because I'm about to talk about circumcision, but like Joan Rivers says, "Can we talk?" We're all grown here!

Now! When this incision is made, it leaves a scar that looks like a ring. Well that's when the revelation came to me that circumcision was done as a covenant, and the cutting away of the flesh was also symbolic of the fact that this was not meant to be used foolishly.

When a child was circumcised, it was symbolic. That particular child just entered into covenant with God. The covenant was stating that the cutting away of excess flesh meant that this person's life was dedicated to God's spiritual purposes and not for fleshly purposes.

It meant that whoever this person was to be joined with had to have the understanding that this individual had a covenant with God. He was able to suffer the pain of coming into covenant, and now he has the ability to come into covenant with me.

This means that the woman who is to experience your ring during sexual intercourse should be *the woman who wears your ring on her finger.* Once she enters into a sexual relationship with you, her life has been changed forever. She will never be able to go back to being who she was before you entered in. There should be an outward sign revealing that you have entered into her life, therefore, you are bonded forever. So the ring on her finger signifies this. Listen my brothers: *don't put a ring in until you put a ring on!*

∞

CIRCUMCISION WAS DONE AS A
COVENANT. THE ONLY WOMAN TO
EXPERIENCE YOUR CIRCUMCISED
RING SHOULD BE THE ONE WEARING
YOUR WEDDING RING.

∞

Not only is sex before marriage painful for the sister, but it's an illegal entry. Anything that is illegal is not subject to proper order; neither can it be subject to commitment. You cannot operate in sex illegally and expect the laws and standards that were meant for marriage to be established in that relationship. Sex before marriage is not bound by any law because it is illegal. This is why an individual can walk out of a relationship anytime he feels like it and not think a second thought about it.

Yeah, the world calls it *common*-law marriage, but is that what you really want? Are you really saying that the women who are adored, loved, and cherished in the eyesight of God and man should be considered just *common?* I don't think so. I think you are much more of a man than that. She's not common; she's special. And if you really feel that she's special—and not just a sexual get-off—then make the decision, "I want her forever to be mine," and marry her!

Understand what I'm about to say and take this in because this is deep, my brothers: There can be no more sheets because having that surgery done was your first step to definition. It said, "I am not a shallow, fleshly man out of control. But, I am a man of depth, wisdom, and commitment."

This is why, my brothers, back in the Bible days, the mother and the father walking under the covenant of God knew the power of being committed and being in right relationship with God. Therefore, from the time their son entered into the world, they prepared him by circumcising him to become a covenant keeper. They were training him from the time he came into the world. When he got old enough to recognize that there had been surgery done on his body, the covenant that he had with God was explained to him.

264

I read in a recent article in *GQ* magazine that during the circumcision of infant males, a painful shock wave goes through their bodies. It was noted that some psychiatrists believe that because of that pain, the male subconsciously grows up protecting that organ. The remembrance of that pain in the nervous system never ends.

This is to be compared with a woman giving birth; that pain is so severe until she almost can't remember just how to describe it. She does remember that it took her as close to death as any human being can ever get. Babies have even died while being circumcised because the shock was so severe that their hearts couldn't take it.

Brothers, why would you use something so powerful and honorable to commit such a dishonorable act on somebody who's not worthy to embrace your covenant? To her, it was a good lay. To her, it was a good get-off; but to God, you've broken a covenant.

Let me ask you a question, my brothers: Does she have virtue, knowledge, temperance, patience, godliness, brotherly kindness, and charity? The Bible states that if she has these things, and these things be in her and abound—meaning that they remain there and meaning that she is consistently operating in these things—she will neither be barren nor unfruitful (see 2 Pet. 1:5-8).

It also states that if any person lacks these things—if these traits are not in them—they will become blind and cannot see afar off (see 2 Pet. 1:9). They have forgotten that they were purged from their old sins. If these things are not abounding in her, she will go back and tamper with old relationships. She will also have desires to be flirtatious and promiscuous.

Daddy Versus Husband

I had to realize one thing, and this one rings a loud bell with me because I was like this in some ways. This is especially for those sisters whose fathers spoiled them rotten and gave them everything they wanted. Every time a man fails to respond to them like their daddy did, it becomes, "You ain't no good."

I had to realize that my daddy was not my husband; he was Daddy. Instead of me paying close attention to all of my dad's ways with my mother as a husband, I was concentrating on everything he was to me as a father. In my mind, I said my husband better treat me just like Daddy did. Boy, was I tricked.

A husband is a husband, and a daddy is a daddy. Let me explain what I mean by that: There were times when I fell out and I pouted and I cried. Even after Daddy told me, "No," he still went out and bought me what I was pouting for.

He did not consider the bills. He did not consider his financial status. He did not consider whether or not I had enough ice cream, or whether or not my mother had just said, "She already had a popsicle" when the ice cream truck came around at six o'clock in the evening. I may have already had a popsicle two hours ago—which my mother felt was enough sweets for the day—but because I cried, Daddy would say, "Oh, let her have it. She just wants some ice cream."

Now, listen to this: When my mother and my father made a decision together, as a husband and wife, to purchase an item, my mother didn't fall out and cry. My father didn't say, "Because you're pouting, I will get it."

They sat down like two adults and they decided. Will this purchase we are about to make interrupt our financial flow? Will it cause us to go in debt? Will we be able to pay the rent? Will we be able to pay the car note and the insurance? Will this interfere with us getting our kids' school clothes?

Do you understand what I mean by a daddy responds like a daddy to a child, but a husband responds to his wife like a husband? This means there must be a certain level of maturity. We cannot afford at this particular stage of our relationships to confuse the two; they are totally separate. And this is why I believe that a woman should not look to find her daddy in her husband, but a woman should look to find a husband of the *Word*.

Many of you may be asking, "Why is she writing such a spiritual book?" My answer to that is there is a demonic force that is causing this nation to rape, molest, and abuse their bodies. Since I know that to be the truth, it will take the power of God to stop it.

This battle is bigger than the human body. This is what we call "the battle of the gods," and God has already won. The battle has been fought. The victory has been won.

I pray that this chapter has been a blessing to your life because I felt really nervous writing it. The more I wrote, the more I began to think, "Forget being nervous. Somebody reading this book could be my next husband." Ha! Ha! Thanks guys, for letting me touch your lives.

CHAPTER THIRTEEN

The Eclipse Is Over

First of all, I'd like to say that if you are still reading this book, and you've made it to the last chapter, you are a brave soldier. I am convinced you really want to be free!

This morning, the Word of the Lord came unto me in a still soft voice saying, "The eclipse is over!" I had never heard anything so soft in my ears, yet it screamed in my spirit so loud until it woke me up, and I sat straight up in the bed, and began to write these words: You must know, today, that your eclipse is over! And because this is such a crucial moment in this book, I need to take a moment to explain this!

There is such a thing in our world and in our atmosphere called a solar eclipse. A solar eclipse is one of the most dramatic sights in the sky. A solar eclipse occurs when the sun seems to vanish. What causes the sun to vanish? The moon comes between the earth and the sun, briefly hiding the sun and casting a shadow on the earth. But, it only lasts for a few minutes. You need to understand the revelation of this.

Many times, there have been things in our lives that have passed between God and us. The moon gets its light from the sun. The moon has been classified as being the same age as the earth.

Now, listen to this: The moon is dry, which means there is nothing to fulfill a thirst. It has no atmosphere, so it cannot support life. Without an atmosphere, there is no weather, the surface is bumpy, there is zero gravity, and anything that goes near it just floats in the atmosphere. Now, isn't that powerful?

Think about how the enemy works when he brings a relationship into your life that is not the will of the Lord. One of the ways that you will begin to judge whether or not you are about to experience a solar eclipse is this: There is no atmosphere, which means that there is no presence of the Lord there. There is no life—meaning the life of the Lord—flowing out of that individual into you or out of you into that individual. It is void.

∾

TAKING AUTHORITY OVER DEMONIC
THOUGHTS CONVEYED BY SATAN IS
NOT A MENTAL EXERCISE, IT IS A
SPIRITUAL WORK.

∾

Now remember: without an atmosphere, there also is no weather and the surface is bumpy, which means that everything in that relationship will always be rocky. When you think one problem is solved, something else is coming up. When you think something else is resolved, here comes something else new.

There's zero gravity, which means there's nothing about this particular relationship that has the ability to hold you steady and hold you firm on the ground. Having both feet on the ground means you're not thinking crazy. Your thoughts are not flighty or immature. You don't allow yourself to do things that will not help you or your spiritual walk with God.

Now, let's look at the operation of the sun. The sun is a violent nuclear reaction constantly taking place. The sun generates energy that spreads out as light and heat and other radiation. Without energy from the sun, life cannot exist on the earth. Isn't that powerful?

Think about this: Without the anointing from the Son of the living God in Christ, life cannot exist on earth. The sun fuses 4 million tons of hydrogen every second. It has enough hydrogen to keep going for 5 billion more years. Half of the sun's energy comes out as light and the other half comes out as heat. Nobody on this earth will ever live to be 5 billion years old. This means that the sun and the power of God can outlive anything that you will ever experience.

It Has to Move

I want you to hear what the Spirit of the Lord is saying to you today about the sun. One of the things that I want to bring out about the sun is that the sun's energy comes out as heat. The sun will consume anything that might happen to float through the sky—anything that would hinder the atmosphere of the earth.

This is the reason why, when the eclipse starts and the moon begins to pass between the sun and the earth, the moon can't stay in that position. *It has to move* out of the way because the power of the sun requires that it keep moving.

The Spirit of the Lord told me to tell you that your eclipse is over. No longer will the enemy bring dead things to stand permanently between you and God. No longer will the enemy be able to hinder the flow of the anointing in your life, or cause you to miss the purpose that God has in store for you. Even if those things come because of the power of sin, the Word says that they can't stay!

You need to recognize by reading this whole book that where I am today in God was not an overnight process. If God brought me out, He's going to bring you out, too. If the Lord delivered me, He's going to deliver you also. God is waiting for you to respond to what He has for you. The decision is left up to you.

The Lord has already given the prophetic word in this book that there will be no more eclipse. Even while you are reading this chapter, the power of the anointing is killing every dead thing that has stepped between you and God. That includes every spirit that is causing you to be unable to serve God the way you desire to—that is, with your whole heart, with your whole mind, and with your whole spirit. I want you to read these final Scriptures God has given me for you. This is going to bless your life:

> *If there is a prophet among you, or one who claims to foretell the future by dreams, and if his predictions come true but he says, "Come, let us worship the gods of the other nations," don't listen to him. For the Lord is testing you to find out whether or not you really love Him with all your heart and soul* (Deuteronomy 13:1-3 TLB).

Now what is God saying right here? When people come and tell you that this is your husband and this is your wife, and what they are prophesying does not line up with scriptural requirements, then the Bible says don't listen to them!

∞

DO YOU REALLY LOVE THE LORD?

∞

The Lord is trying to find out whether or not you're going to be led away because you're burning in your flesh. Are you going to grab the first little prophecy that comes along because it agrees with your flesh? Remember I said your flesh, not your spirit!

How Will You Recognize an Eclipse?

You must never worship any God but Jehovah; obey only His commands and cling to Him. The prophet who tries to lead you astray must be executed, for he has attempted to foment rebellion against the Lord your God who brought you out of slavery in the land of Egypt. By executing him you will clear out the evil from among you. If your nearest relative or closest friend, even a brother, son, daughter, or beloved wife whispers to you to come and worship these foreign gods, do not consent or listen, and have no pity: do not spare that person from the penalty; don't conceal his horrible suggestion. Execute him! Your own hand shall be the first upon him to put him to death, then the hands of all the people. Stone him to death because he has tried to draw you away from the Lord your God who brought you from the land of Egypt, the place of slavery. Then all Israel will hear about his evil deed and will fear such wickedness as this among you. If you ever hear it said about one of the cities of Israel that some worthless rabble have led their fellow citizens astray with the suggestion that they worship foreign gods, first check the facts to see if the rumor is true. If you find that it is, that it is certain that such a horrible thing is happening among you in one of the cities the Lord has given you, you must without fail declare war against that city and utterly destroy all of its inhabitants, and even all of the cattle (Deuteronomy 13:4-15 TLB).

In other words, by killing that spirit, you will clear out the evil from among you. The Bible says to execute him; that means kill him. That means kill the thing that's coming against you.

It also states that the person who's trying to draw you away from the will of God should be rebuked. Disconnect yourself from him. You've been a slave too long. You've been in Egypt too long. You've been bound up too long. You've been in the sheets too long. When God begins to deliver you, He's saying that this vengeance you ought to have in your spirit now: "I will kill and destroy any spirit in anybody that comes against me, trying to drag me back to that slavery."

∞

DISCONNECT YOURSELF FROM THOSE
WHO TRY TO DRAW YOU AWAY FROM
THE WILL OF GOD.

∞

This Means War!

If you hear about someone trying to convince other people by saying, "It ain't nothing wrong with this. It ain't nothing wrong with petting. It ain't nothing wrong with kissing. It ain't nothing wrong with feeling. It ain't nothing wrong with sneaking every now and then. Everybody ought to test the goods before they get married." The Bible said to first find out if that's true. If you find that it is, that this thing has happened among you in one of the cities (the church that you go to), then you must declare war against that spirit. Afterward, you must gather all of the spoils.

And thou shalt gather all the spoil of it into the midst of the street thereof, and shalt burn with fire the city, and all the spoil thereof every whit, for the Lord thy God: and it shall be an heap for ever; it shall not be built again (Deuteronomy 13:16).

That was one of the first things that I had to do when I decided to declare war against that spirit. I had to war with being entangled again with that bondage. Remember when I brought everything out in the floor that individuals had bought me and I gave it away? I got rid of it. I gave a brand-new car that I paid off to one of my sisters. I didn't want it.

Once you've been freed from slavery, why do you still want the shackles? Once you've been freed from bondage, why do you still want the chains? There's got to be something wrong with you to be released from prison, but still desire to take the jail bars with you. Listen to this my brothers and sisters:

Keep none of the booty! Then the Lord will turn from His fierce anger and be merciful to you, and have compassion upon you, and make you a great nation just as He promised your ancestors. Of course, the Lord your God will be merciful only if you have been obedient to Him and to His commandments that I am giving you today, and if you have been doing that which is right in the eyes of the Lord (Deuteronomy 13:17-18 TLB).

What a powerful Scripture! When you purpose in your heart that you're tired of the sheets in your life, you will get rid of all of the spoils. You will allow God to purify your temple. And you will use the Word to stay sober, to be vigilant, and to be focused.

❦

WHY WOULD YOU STILL WANT THE
CHAINS? GET RID OF EVERYTHING
THAT REPRESENTS THE BONDAGE
YOU WERE IN—CLOTHES, JEWELRY,
FURNITURE—*EVERYTHING*.

❦

Use everything that God has put around you—the counsel of the elders and the authority of leadership. Only then will you be able to recognize that the Lord is restoring you back to your place in Him. At this point, you can boldly declare, *"There will be no more sheets."*

Right now, as you finish the final words in this book, I feel strongly in my spirit that the deliverance will be *no more sheets*.

God bless you. My brothers and sisters, I love you dearly and *the Lord loves you too!*

CHAPTER FOURTEEN

Starting Over

Wow! I can see now that I've been true to my own words in the original text of *No More Sheets*. What I said at the time was that, if I ever found myself in the same predicament again, I would take my own advice and read my own book and listen to my own tapes (or CDs in today's world) and start all over again.

And here I am. Do I feel ashamed? No, I do not. Do I feel helpless and hopeless? Absolutely not. To be honest, I feel empowered. I feel stronger than I did on the day I first stood on the platform and preached this message to more than 15,000 people.

As you were reading the book through, you probably said, "Wow. How can she stand so strong and confident given all that she has gone through over the course of the past few years?"

I think the answer depends on which side of the fence you choose to stand, or how you choose to see the glass. Do you see the glass half full or half empty?

In looking back over the years since I first preached "No More Sheets," and especially over more recent events in my life, I think I would say what my grandmother used to say: "I wouldn't take nothing from my journey, and if God gave me an opportunity to do it all over again, I wouldn't change nothing."

The reason I'd ask of Him to change nothing is this: Anytime you encounter trouble or tragedy, if you will just wait and be still long enough, you'll find valuable new information hidden somewhere in the midst of it all. It is a new level of power being placed into your hands.

Many people have a tendency to spend the rest of their lives focusing on how bad it felt and how bad it hurt. They get hung up on the pain and never, ever, ever allow themselves to get to the end of the transition.

∞

WHEN YOU RENEW YOUR MIND ON A CONTINUAL BASIS, YOU ACTUALLY BEGIN TO REPLACE OLD THOUGHTS WITH NEW THOUGHTS.

∞

When people would look at me and say, "Oh my God! She is in so much trouble!" I would abruptly stop them and say, "I am not in trouble. I'm in transition."

It took me awhile to get to that place, but when I finally did, it was up to me, not other people, to define the state I was in. Why? Because by the time I got to where I had any form of personal communication with people, the real root of the trouble had already been revealed to me.

I was made to understand that trouble was the thing God was going to use to transition me from one place to the next. That was the process I could expect when He saw that His intended purpose for my life was "stuck."

In the beginning, people began saying that I was called to the nations. I took that in the sense of the traditional church arena, and it had a powerful sound to it. It was only recently that I began to understand clearly that Christendom accounts for a small percentage of the world's population! I understood that, if God called me to *all the world*, I wasn't there yet. So far, I had been celebrated in a place that was my training ground, not my destiny.

After mounting major platforms and writing books and conducting my own conferences with thousands of people attending, for some reason that I could not explain, I felt stuck. I recognized that all that I had accomplished still gave me the feeling that I had not reached destiny. I began to see that I had become just as segregated as everybody else, yet with arms opened wide and a heart that was willing to reach the world.

Still, I realized that I did not have the proper tools, so I began to ask myself, "What is it that causes a person to be able to reach the world? What are the ingredients needed for an individual to touch hearts beyond their circle and beyond their race and beyond their religion?"

I believe it is the common denominator that links us all; it is the one thing that is partial to neither race nor religion: it's a little something called *pain!* Pain is pain. It is not white pain or black pain or Asian pain. It's not African or Episcopalian or Catholic or Church of God in Christ pain. It's not even limited to Christianity. Pain is about people; it is felt by people everywhere, all standing under the same sky and the same sun and going to bed under the same moon.

Pain affects anyone and everyone who has a heart beating in their chest and a soul troubled within them and a mind they can't seem to calm. It is then and only then that you can identify with the world; it is then and only then that you can see through the world's eyes to be able to understand that we are all essentially the same.

What makes us different from one another and what causes one to be a cut "above" another is choice—not just the choice itself, but the opportunity to be given a choice. I believe that so many people live in pain and discontent submerged in a life full of chaos for a very simple reason: few people make it to the other side of pain. Few have transitioned to the point of being able to turn around (*because* of what they have experienced) and offer others the opportunity to choose.

I believe that in choosing to resurrect this book and write this chapter called "Starting Over," that is exactly what I did. I chose to write this chapter to initiate a thought pattern. I realize that I may not be able to get you to turn around at this very moment. I may not even be able to get you to stop hurting from the inside this very second; but what I can offer you is choice.

When trouble came calling a very few years ago, I began to research and try with everything in me to do what I've always done when trouble comes—I went to God in prayer, and I went to the Church. It's what I'd done for 20 years. Yet, when I tried all of that and I did all of that, the pain wouldn't stop. This time, for some reason, when I went into my prayer room and cried out to God, it was as though God were a million miles away from me. When I put on my white robe and lay on the floor, I felt nothing.

I began to ask myself whether this pain was real and whether it was the same pain shared by those who listen when I'm standing in the pulpit—the ones who come hurting when I have

45 minutes to an hour to call down the presence of God and give someone the opportunity to stand in that presence and be healed...or delivered...or uplifted.

In that 45 minutes to an hour when I might not even be able to complete the message, they are asked to try with everything that is within them to grab hold of a piece of change and a sliver of choice so that they can go home and try—within the realm of who they are and in the atmosphere in which they are living—to find peace of mind.

Was that the same pain I was feeling?

Now that it was my turn, I knew that I was in the same predicament as the next person. Forget about the fact that I was a preacher or a prophet or an evangelist or a doctor or teacher; at that moment, I was just a person in pain. I turned to what I knew from the traditional form of church and I couldn't find help for my pain.

I searched high and low and couldn't find help. I think the thing that really shook me more than anything was the fact that I was ready—ready to try everything I could to press past it all. Yet, I was being told by bishops and preachers that my life was over and my ministry was finished. They laughed at me from boardrooms with comments like, "He took her down."

And all those who did reach out—I could feel that there was only so much they would say or do because everybody had allegiances. How was I going to get help from a bishop when my abuser was a bishop? Who would be willing to step beyond their inner circle, not to take my side, but to stand up for what was right?

As I waited, I finally had to accept the fact that I was on my own and that, if I were going to make it, it would be by the mercy of God. I had to find a way to silence the words being spoken into my spirit: "You might as well go to another country. You need to hide out. You need to stop preaching because it's over for you."

I sat in my prayer room under the weight of all of these words. While the press ripped me apart on the outside, I was attacked on every hand. I was the victim, and all of a sudden I was being treated as though I had attacked or done harm to myself. After 25 years of investing my life to minister to so many people, I suddenly felt like the most alone person in the world.

And, yes, even thoughts of suicide and attempts at suicide came. Yet, it was at that moment and at that hour that I received a message from someone who wasn't even a part of the Church, someone who had no claims to the Holy Spirit or the Gospel. Still, the message came clearly: "Never put your microphone down! Never stop preaching! Never give up who God has called you to become!"

After hearing those words, I began this journey again. After losing everything and feeling like I was left alone, I had just two friends who would hold my hand. Neither of them were people of "status" in the Church. What they had was the heart and soul of everyday people moved by the sight of someone lying wounded at the roadside. They had the heart to say, "We'll give you a hand and help you make it through, even if it costs us our own lives!" And they did just that!

Suddenly, I realized that I had to stop and ask God to help me and show me and give me an answer—not just an answer for me, but an answer for every person in the kind of pain I was experiencing. I wanted answers, because in my heart of hearts I wouldn't wish that kind of pain on my worst enemy!

One of the first things He said to me was, "Juanita Bynum, you are not in trouble; you are in transition. And I will tell you how and I will tell you why, because you are now living the life of millions and millions of others. When I am finished transitioning you, you will have a revelation. You will have an answer that will bring many out of where they are, and they too will begin to start their lives all over again."

The first thing I had to do was to not be afraid to face head on every situation and condition of my present state. I think a lot of times, when we look at words such as *negative...trouble... tragedy...*or *chaos* from a natural standpoint (depending on how much knowledge we have or how far we are able to pursue more knowledge), we often live our lives by the surface level of the word's definition.

In reality, we know that for everything that is stated, there is a deeper meaning. There is a deeper revelation, just as is true with the Word of God. Certainly, I can remember the first time I read the verse that says, *"Jesus wept"* (John 11:35); but after three years of my transition, that particular Scripture began to weigh in heavier than it did when I was a kindergartener saying it in Sunday school.

As you begin to mature, you experience things on different levels. Then the meaning of the Word—even the Scriptures you have known all your life—contain the power to change you. Suddenly, a simple passage will cause you to transcend to a deeper place of revelation.

Allow me to explain this a little further. The first thought you have when you hear the word *trouble* opens you up to the perspective of chaos. You become shaken and out of sorts. That's the way that I was during my first year of transition, until one day when I was in prayer and meditation and received the unction from God to look up the word *trouble*.

I looked it up and found that the word *trouble* means "a condition of pain, disease, or malfunction: *heart trouble; car trouble*." Another definition means "unrest and a disorder." When I saw that yet another definition was "a personal habit or trait" that is likely to incur problems or difficulties—"a cause of mental distress," I said, "Wow!"[1]

So, in other words, when a person understands that they are experiencing *trouble*, trouble turns into *transition*. Why? Because the trouble brings you face to face with information from within. This information in turn empowers you to understand that there is a malfunction somewhere in your life. You realize that the unrest you are experiencing is the result of something that is out of order.

That's right, when you begin to experience trouble, it is your first sign that something in your life needs to stop. You become aware that the reason you are having a malfunction and experiencing chaos is because something is simply out of order.

When I understood this, it gave me a way out of the trouble. Instead of living in the hype of my emotions, I began to turn myself, slowly but surely. It wasn't easy, and it wasn't instant; but it was doable, and I began to practice it. Every time something else hit me, I would say, "OK. This is out of order," or "OK. I need to realign myself with the divine order of God for my life."

I began to recognize what I should pursue and what I should never, ever look back to again. When I saw the golden opportunity I was being given to recognize disorder and put things back in alignment, I knew that I was in control and able to bring all of it to a halt.

As I continued to study the word *trouble*, something caught me that I had never really paid attention to in the past. I began to recognize that trouble presents a choice. It is not only negative; it has a positive side, too. So I began to say, "OK. Let me learn what the negatives will be if I stay on the wrong side of this thing. What is ahead if I don't take this opportunity to bring order to whatever is malfunctioning? How can I align myself with God's ways so that I don't experience even more difficulty in this area? What can I expect if I refuse to 'line up' and opt to wallow in pain?"

I realized that, unless I bring order, I am choosing to embrace the negative side of trouble and all that comes with it, including refusal and rejection and unresponsiveness and opposing opinions and detriment and contradiction. Everything I did or didn't do would result in outcomes that contradict who God says I really am.

One of the keys in this revelation is this: When something negative is spoken and when negativity surrounds us, it becomes a statement of position that is opposite to what God has said about us. If we have been created by God (and we were!), then He is the One who spoke all things into existence. Therefore, the reason there is a negative situation is that the negative is coming against the positive—which is whatever God has spoken over us.

In other words, there can be no negative without a positive. The negative has to have something to push against. It is the will of the enemy for us never to understand who God has called us to be and who we are to become. We must understand that in God's eyes we are already who He has called us to be! We are already complete and finished in Him; that's why the negativity comes—to get us emotionally and mentally and physically out of order so that we miss our divine purpose.

∾

You are complete in God, not man.

∾

When you look at all that negativity entails, you will see that one of the words used to describe negativity is the word *proscription*. A proscription is "an imposed restraint or restriction."[2]

When you are a negative person you are writing yourself a proscription, a denunciation, a ban and barring which leads to public condemnation. When you choose to live on the negative side of your life and experiences (seeing only how you were hurt and how the pain is still there), then you are agreeing that you are going to be refused; you are agreeing that you are going to be rejected. You have positioned yourself to be banned and barred; you have positioned yourself to live the rest of your life in public condemnation.

You may be asking yourself, "How can I turn that around, Dr. Bynum? How can I start again?"

You can start again by recognizing that you have the power to turn it around through spiritual knowledge. The Bible tells us that it is knowledge that digs up the depths.

When I dug a little deeper I saw the pivotal point of this entire puzzle. I saw that if a person really wanted destiny, this would be the one thing that could give that person the power to turn it around!

It is the fact that the word *trouble* can also denote the effort it takes to do something, especially when it is inconvenient. In other words, you "go to some trouble" to turn the situation around. How you turn trouble into transition is by choosing to stand and move on who you know you have been called to become—even when it's inconvenient.

That's right! When the tears are coming and you are feeling depressed, you have to recognize that the actions and events opposing you are designed to produce the opposite result of who you know God has called you to be!

When you see this, it is your responsibility to make a statement and a stand, even in the midst of the opposing fact. Why? Because the difference between negative and positive is found in a word related to the word *positive;* it is the word *prescription*. It means you write yourself a prescription—you recommend a substance or action that will be beneficial to you. It means "to state authoritatively or as a rule that an action or procedure should and will be carried out."[3]

When you look at the opportunity that you are being given, you have to keep your eyes on it—on the prescription—and not on the opposition! You cannot look at the negative without recognizing and respecting the fact that somewhere beneath it all, there is a positive waiting for you: it's an opportunity to write your own prescription.

The Scripture mentions the ancient proverb, "Physician, heal thyself" (see Luke 4:23). When Jesus quoted that proverb, He was being sarcastic. Without God, we can't be healed. But we have the ultimate physician:

> *If you will listen to the voice of the Lord your God and obey it, and do what is right, then I will not make you suffer the diseases I sent on the Egyptians, for I am the Lord who heals you* (Exodus 15:26 TLB).

There it is: He has written the prescription. It becomes your responsibility to digest it on a daily basis. You are going to take this substance into your spirit like you would take a medicine into your body.

Once the prescription is written, it is the responsibility of God to fill the prescription. We must take the step; we must move; we must take the medicine. He moves according to what we speak. Remember the Scripture that says that death and life are in the power of the tongue? (See Proverbs 18:21.)

The Scripture that says when you pay your vow…when you adhere to who you have been called to be…when you begin to move toward that action…when you yield and take instruction from His mouth—then the Word said you can decree a thing (see Job 22:21-28). Another translation says you can then decide a thing and it will come to pass (see Job 22:28 NIV).

I am a living witness to the fact that I have seen more trouble than I would probably ever need to see for the rest of my life. I am one to say I have experienced enough trouble in recent years to pass around to the world and still have some left over. Even so, I had to come to the point of seeking wisdom and knowledge rather than someone to feel sorry for me. I had to finally realize that my healing wasn't going to come from religion, but from a newfound relationship with the Spirit of wisdom and knowledge.

It is difficult for some people to grab the fact that you can stand in the atmosphere of the sanctuary and lift your hands up and the presence of God will do a new thing in your heart.

∞

WORSHIP IS WHAT TRANSPORTS YOU
INTO THE PRESENCE OF GOD. HIS
PRESENCE IS WHAT HELPS YOU TO
DEFINE WHO YOU ARE AND WHO
GOD IS.

∞

If I get under that presence and I receive a sense of healing, for *that moment* I walk in and feel the presence of peace and the presence of joy.

How do I maintain that in my everyday life? What we are looking for in the endtimes is not just an instant experience. We're not looking for something momentary; we're looking for something for a lifetime.

∞

YOUR SPIRITUAL RELATIONSHIP
WITH GOD SHOULD ALWAYS BE THE
ULTIMATE JOY IN YOUR LIFE.

∞

We're not looking to just stand in the sanctuary and receive something that we could never use once we walk out of the four walls of the church. Because once we receive that presence, we have to have knowledge as to how we can take that presence and write ourselves a prescription. We need to learn how to survive after the choir and the drummer have gone home, after the pianist and organist have left the building. We have to know how to survive even when we have no access to the pastor and no elders are there to pray for us.

How Do I Survive?

You survive through the wisdom and knowledge of God. That's why the Bible says, *"with all thy getting get understanding"* (Prov. 4:7). That wisdom is to be desired more than gold. Even more than you desire great wealth, you must desire wisdom, because it is through wisdom that you will transition in life and become a person who evolves and evolves and keeps on evolving until you reach your destiny.

289

Where we are headed is the place where we are not afraid when the negative comes; we're not afraid when we see trouble, because we know that when trouble comes, transition is possible. Trouble means transition and transition means I'm being given the opportunity to recognize that something positive has already been established in me.

Negativity comes against a positive that is already there, which means the promise is already there. Therefore, negativity tells me that this thing is coming to try to ban me and keep me away from what is already mine. I know when negativity comes that I am being given an opportunity to write myself a prescription, digest it on a daily basis, and recommend something to my soul that will benefit me for a lifetime!

I now have the power to speak authoritatively and state a rule or an action or a procedure that will be carried out by me, which then gives me the power that I need to start all over again.

Even though you may see this chapter as being the end of this book, it is more than that. It is the beginning, a brand-new start for you. Why? Because as the song says, "It ain't over until God says it's over!"

Once again, you are being given the chance to say with me:

"This is my life and if I don't like it, I will change it!"

Decree now:

"No more sheets! No more sheets! *No more sheets!*

Endnotes

1.   Dictionary.com, s.v. "trouble," http://dictionary.reference.com/browse/trouble.

2. Dictionary.com. Merriam-Webster's Dictionary of Law. Merriam-Webster, Inc., s.v. "proscription," http://dictionary.reference.com/browse/proscription (accessed: January 06, 2010).

3. Dictionary.com. Merriam-Webster's Dictionary of Law. Merriam-Webster, Inc., s.v. "prescription," http://dictionary.reference.com/browse/prescription (accessed: January 06, 2010).

REFLECTIONS

REFLECTIONS

REFLECTIONS

REFLECTIONS

Reflections

REFLECTIONS

REFLECTIONS

REFLECTIONS

Author Contact

Juanita Bynum Ministries

Post Office Box 162426
Atlanta, GA 30321

Phone: 1-866-942-9686

www.juanitabynum.com